FOOD SAFETY IN KITCHEN

KITCHEN HYGIENE & SANITIZER

CHEF SATHISHKUMAR SOMASUNDARAM

Made with ♥ on the Notion Press Platform
www.notionpress.com

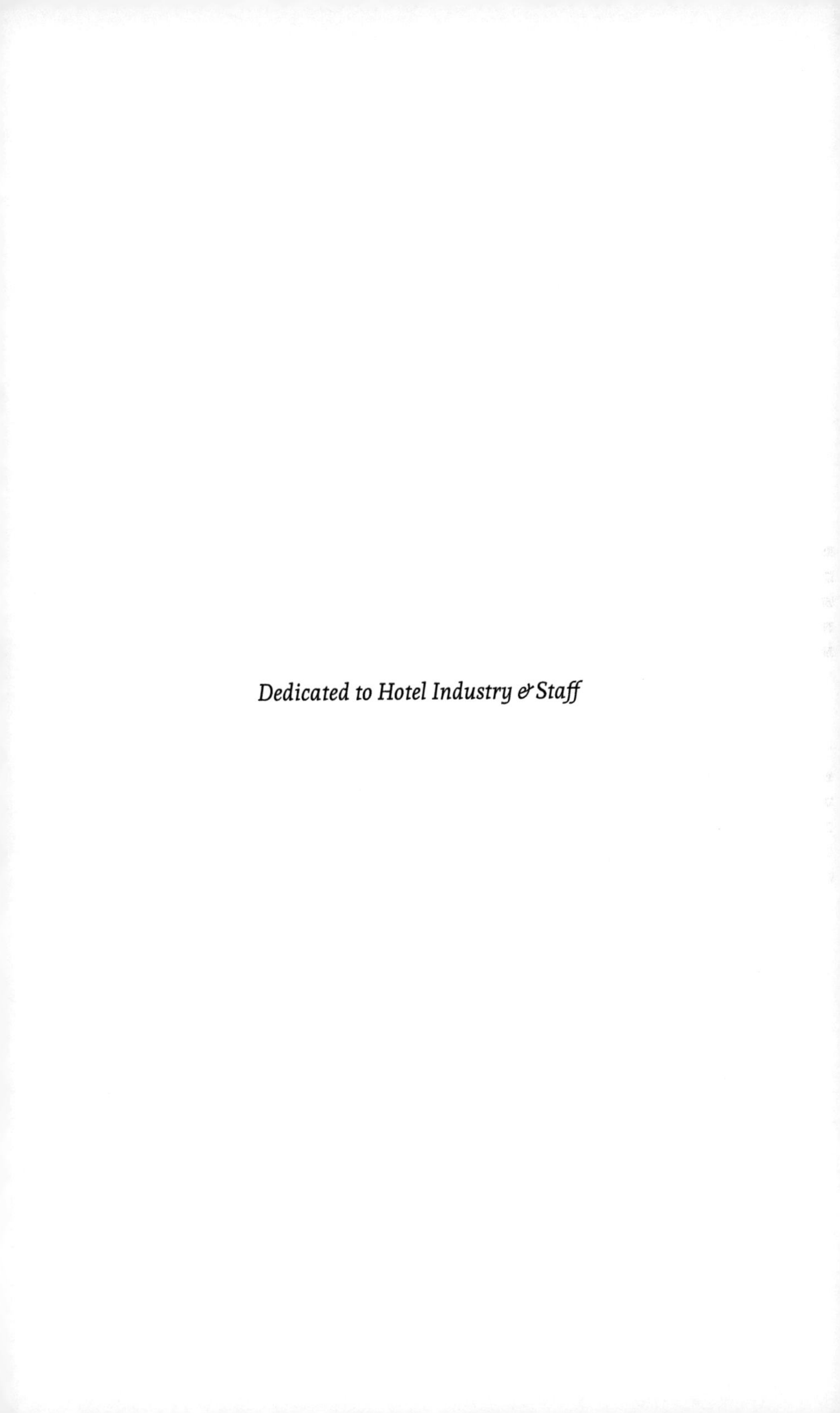

Dedicated to Hotel Industry & Staff

Contents

FOREWORD

This book provides a widely useful compilation of ideas, cases, innovative approaches, and practical strategies for enhancing a little-discussed school activity—Food Safety in Kitchen. By taking a new look at these ubiquitous programs, Anne Turnbaugh Lockwood identifies a substantial resource in the effort to increase student learning. In this book he provides an enormously useful range of strategies for designing, implementing, and evaluating Food Safety in Kitchen. This work would be an important resource if it only highlighted the ways Food Safety in Kitchen, could enrich their missions by establishing academics as a more central part of their work. But the book goes well beyond just making us aware of this seemingly underutilized learning setting. It covers and describes all the major factors in building successful Food Safety in Kitchen that enhance achievement. This volume is an important resource for school principals, agencies that provide Food Safety in Kitchen, districts, and parent groups whose children use these services. First, it provides a new perspective on Food Safety in Kitchen, showing how they can be an important source for both recreation and academic learning. Food Safety in Kitchen is found all across the United States serving millions of students. Understanding how they can more effectively serve the learning needs of students adds a major cache of time for helping all students achieve. Second, the book provides a relevant and constructive set of strategies and ideas for making these programs effective. Numerous research studies, Internet Web sites, and publications extend these ideas. This book should be read by anyone who views Food Safety in Kitchen as an additional way to help students learn, because it offers a wide set of practical ideas for designing, implementing, and evaluating these programs. All the key processes necessary for changing an existing or implementing a new program are found in this volume. ix any leader who wants to develop effective Food Safety in Kitchen that foster student learning will gain much from this book. For example, the reader is offered concrete examples of effective programs through case studies of existing afterschool efforts. These cases show what a good program looks like, how it is run, and key features. In addition, the book lays out practical steps for planning programs, hiring staff, designing curriculum, selecting activities, and providing professional development. In another section, Lockwood lists an important set of issues to consider when designing an afterschool program and then adds an inventory of important questions to consider. She describes barriers to success and then presents suggestions for overcoming those barriers. Throughout the book, Lockwood sets out to make the material accessible to readers interested in implementing these programs—these ideas are found in the form of questions and suggestions, tables of issues to address, and practical strategies to consider. The tables and strategies themselves are worth the price of the book. This book also examines several other issues that often spell the end of quality programs—developing a parent and community base of support, designing adequate program evaluation processes, and planning for sustainability. One finds a useful set of questions, ideas, and strategies for building a base of support among parents and the community. The section on program evaluation is quite practical and detailed. It offers a clear description of ways schools can and should evaluate Food Safety in Kitchen. Finally, the book on sustainability details challenges to the viability of Food Safety in Kitchen and suggests actions should take to ensure that these programs are successful in the long term. Overall, this book offers a variety of hotel and Food leaders a concrete, useful, and in-depth look at ways to design, implement, and evaluate a major resource in the learning of students. Clearly written, well organized, and enormously practical, it should be in every chef's professional library.

Chef Sathishkumar Somasundaram
Assistant Professor
Department of Catering Science and Hotel Management
Nehru Arts and Science Collage –Coimbatore

T.R Rajesh Pandian
Head of Department
Department of Catering Science and Hotel Management
Nehru Arts and Science Collage –Coimbatore
Date 12.22.2022

Preface

I realize that this book will create a great deal of Food handler. It has never been easy to challenge the consensus because the System – of any kind, in any context – will try to preserve the status quo, by all means possible. Having spent 19 years in the field of hotel management as a chef. I feel obliged to share my knowledge, analyses, and conclusions. Hopefully, this book will raise the level of awareness among the general public and students initiate the discussion that, in turn, may entail major cultural changes, as well as a revision of the consumer basket. The beneficiaries will be all of us – ourselves, our children, our beloved ones, and the society, as a whole – who will live a healthier, and longer, life. I would like the food consumption to be not a routine procedure for gaining nutrients that the body needs, but a science-based process with complete predictability of its overall impact and fate of every food component entering the human body. Throughout, the book has been written with this audience in mind. At times, the science presented might seem overwhelming: busy schemes with multiple structures, electrons movements, charges, and intimidating chemical names. I hope that you won't be easily discouraged are very light in chemistry and can be easily understood by a layperson. One of the important features of this book is that it does not have a textbook structure when the chapters, the group of readers will be represented by professionals from the food industry, academia, and government agencies, as well as consumer protection. But I do hope that the information and knowledge presented will become a wake-up call for the general public, regulatory agencies, legislators, business leaders, coming to the realization that the current state of affairs is not satisfactory, to say the least, and it needs to be fixed .I hope this book is widely read. If we are to avoid the blunders of the past, then we need to change the direction and start benefiting from the knowledge base created by the food handler. We did not have this chance a decade ago. Now is the right time.

Chef Sathishkumar Somasundaram
Assistant Professor
Department of Catering Science and Hotel Management
Nehru Arts and Science Collage –Coimbatore
T.R Rajesh Pandian
Head of Department
Department of Catering Science and Hotel Management
Nehru Arts and Science Collage –Coimbatore
Date 12.22.2022

ACKNOWLEDGEMENTS

Like many authors who wrote about Food Safety in Kitchen before me, I want to express my thanks and admiration to the group of visionaries who invented Food Safety in Kitchen and to those who keep extending it creatively and applying it to new domains. I am very grateful to the many readers of the preliminary forms of the manuscript who taught me a lot by their criticism and suggested ideas that are now implemented in the text. I am also obliged to my students whose blank looks alerted me to inappropriate presentation strategies and whose improvements of classroom examples served to improve the text. I hope that I will get similar constructive suggestions for improvements from the readers of this book as well. Finally, I must acknowledge the influence of the Food Safety in Kitchen news group on Internet at comp.lang.Food Safety in Kitchen. I learned a lot from it and borrowed some of the ideas expressed at this forum for examples and exercises. I have been teaching Food Safety for the last five years and forgotten many of the students who actively shaped my understanding of Food Safety in Kitchen and influenced my teaching, I wish Thanks to Google.com and Fssai of India Also wish to thank the following Family and friends whose names stand out in my memory. Most of them are now employed as professional Food Safety in Kitchen programmers. Finally, but most importantly, I wish to thank my family. During the long time that it took to write this book, my wife Saranaya managed to pretend that spending the time that other people devote to holidays on my computer was a part of normal life, smoothed over my continuous swings between fascination and frustration with this book, and added a human dimension to my life. My two children - Ivan, Vishnu and Vishwa – helped greatly to maintain this illusion. I have been very lucky to have a family that provided such a warm, supportive, and stimulating environment.

I wish to thank my College and Management (NASC Family)

Prologue

Like many authors who wrote about Food Safety in Kitchen before me, I want to express my thanks and admiration to the group of visionaries who invented Food Safety in Kitchen and to those who keep extending it creatively and applying it to new domains. I am very grateful to the many readers of the preliminary forms of the manuscript who taught me a lot by their criticism and suggested ideas that are now implemented in the text. I am also obliged to my students whose blank looks alerted me to inappropriate presentation strategies and whose improvements of classroom examples served to improve the text. I hope that I will get similar constructive suggestions for improvements from the readers of this book as well. Finally, I must acknowledge the influence of the Food Safety in Kitchen news group on Internet at comp.lang.Food Safety in Kitchen. I learned a lot from it and borrowed some of the ideas expressed at this forum for examples and exercises. I have been teaching Food Safety for the last five years and forgotten many of the students who actively shaped my understanding of Food Safety in Kitchen and influenced my teaching, I wish Thanks to Google.com and Fssai of India Also wish to thank the following Family and friends whose names stand out in my memory.

I

Food Safety

"Food is your medicine, and your medicine is you food"

- "Chef Sathishkumar

Food Safety : Importance of safety – Accidents from structural inadequacies – Accidents from improper placemen of equipment in spaces – Accidents due to nature and behaviour of people at work – Accidents from improper selection, installation, maintenance and storage of equipment – Safety procedure – Training – Safety engineering – Enforcement of safety – Safety education

Food Safety Food safety means assurance that food is acceptable for human consumption according to its intended use. An understanding of food safety is improved by defining two other concepts — toxicity and hazard. Toxicity is the capacity of a substance to produce harm or injury of any kind under any conditions. Hazard is the relative probability that harm or injury will result when substance is not used in a prescribed manner and quantity. Hazards can be physical, chemical and biological causing harmful / adverse effects on the health of consumers.

Physical hazard is any physical material not normally found in food, which causes illness or injury and includes wood, stones, parts of pests, hair etc.

Chemical hazards in foods Chemical hazards are chemicals or deleterious substances which may be intentionally or unintentionally added to foods. This category of hazards includes pesticides, chemical residues, toxic metals, polychlorinated biphenyls, preservatives, food colours and other additives

Biological hazards are living organisms and include microbiological organisms

Those micro-organisms which are associated with food and cause diseases are termed food-borne pathogens. There are two types of food-borne diseases from microbial pathogens—infections and poisoning.

Food Poisoning results from ingestion of live pathogenic organisms which multiply in the body and cause disease. Salmonella is a classic example. This organism exists in the intestinal tract of animals. Raw milk and eggs are also sources. Heat destroys Salmonella; however, inadequate cooking allows some organisms to survive. Often Salmonella is spread through cross-contamination. This could happen when a cook cuts raw meat/ poultry on a chopping board and without cleaning uses it for another food which does not involve any cooking, such as salad. Food may become infected by Salmonella if an infected food handler does not wash hands with soap after using bathroom and before touching food. Salmonella can reproduce very quickly and double their number every 20 minutes. The symptoms of Salmonella infection include diarrheal, fever and abdominal cramps. Food intoxication: Some bacteria produce harmful toxins which are present in food even if pathogen has been killed. Organisms produce toxins when the food has not been hot enough or cold enough. Toxins in food cannot be detected by smell, appearance or taste. Hence foods which smell and appear good are not necessarily safe. One example of such an organism is Staphylococcus aureus. Such organisms exist in air, dust, water. They are also present in the nasal passage, throat and on skin, hair of 50 per cent of healthy individuals. People who carry this organism, contaminate food if they touch these places on body while food handling. Diarrheal is also one of the symptoms of this contamination. Parasites can also cause infestation, e.g., worm infestation by tape worm in pork. In addition to this, food can be infested by pests and insects Infestation of foods among the various hazards, biological hazards are an important cause of food-borne illnesses. In spite of all the efforts in the area of food safety, microbial food-borne pathogens are still a serious concern and new pathogens continue to emerge. Factors that are important in the emergence of pathogens include human host, animal hosts and their interactions with humans, the pathogen itself, and the environment including how food is produced, processed, handled and stored. For example, changes in host susceptibility due to malnutrition, age and other conditions can allow for the emergence of new infections in vulnerable populations. Genetic exchange or mutations in the organisms can create new strains with the potential to cause disease. Exposure to new pathogens through changes in eating habits, climate, mass production, food processing and increased globalisation of the food supply can allow pathogens to emerge in new populations or new geographic areas. Examples are Norovirus, Rotavirus, hepatitis E contributing to about 70 per cent of cases. New pathogens will continue to evolve and there is a need to develop methods to isolate them, control them and detect their presence in foods. In the context of food safety, it is important to understand the terms contamination and adulteration. Contamination: It is the presence of harmful or objectionable foreign substances in food such as chemicals, micro-organisms, and dilutants before/during or after processing or storage. Adulteration: Food adulteration is the process in which the quality of food is lowered either by the addition of inferior quality material or by extraction of valuable ingredient. It not only includes the intentional addition or substitution of the substances but biological and chemical contamination during the period of growth, storage, processing, transport and distribution of the food products. It is also responsible for lowering or degradation of the quality of food products. Adulterants: are those substances which are used for making the food products unsafe for human consumption. Having understood what food safety is, let us discuss food quality.

Food Quality: The term food quality refers to attributes that influence a product's value to consumers. This includes both negative attributes such as spoilage, contamination, adulteration, food safety hazards as well as positive attributes such as colour, flavour, texture. It is therefore a holistic concept integrating factors such as nutritional traits, sensorial properties (colour, texture, shape, appearance, taste, flavour, and odour), social considerations, safety. Safety is a preliminary attribute and precursor of quality. In order to ensure that foods are safe and of good quality, across the world various governments and international bodies have laid down food standards that manufacturers/suppliers are expected to adhere to. Thus, all food service providers (those involved at all stages of pre-preparation and preparation/processing, packaging and service) should adhere to good manufacturing practices and ensure food safety.

Salient points to be borne in mind are:

1. Quality of raw materials and water

2. Cleanliness — of the premises, personnel, equipment, food preparation and storage and serving areas 3. Storage of food at appropriate temperature

4. Food hygiene

5. Good service practices.

Safety

While attention to safety is important in all areas of a catering establishment, the one most vulnerable to accidents and therefore injuries is the kitchen. This is because it is the centre where a variety of fuels are used; and a number of people with different mental and physical abilities work together. Besides, they handle large volumes of food often at steaming temperatures; lift heavy equipment; use sharp tools and often work under pressure especially during peak periods. Service and storage areas for food provide enough temptations for pilferage and theft which therefore needs to be guarded against if an establishment is to prove financially viable.'

Every catering establishment therefore, needs to develop a safety policy which ensures protection to property, equipment, materials and people within the establishment at all times, whether staff, customers, or visitors. In order to do this a detailed appraisal of all possible safety hazards is necessary.

Accidents may result from a number of causes-physical, psychological or environmental leading to falls, cuts, shocks, burns, collision at work and many more.

1. **Accidents from Structural Inadequacies:** All structural designing should aim at a smooth work flow in every area of a catering establishment. To prevent accidents

    1. The presence of 'blind comers' or cross-traffic aisles increasing the chances of accidents by collision.
    2. When the level of floors is uneven, causing people to trip and fall.
    3. When floor coverings are not fixed properly and provide crevices and cracks causing falls due to tripping. Too smooth or shiny flooring can cause slips too. Concrete floors are safer in terms of fire hazard than wooden ones with coverings.
    4. If spaces are too small for the activities to be performed in them, it leads to overcrowding, noise and confusion, leading to physical and mental stress. The results can be collision, injury through breakages and much more.
    5. When doors open on to work areas they can hit people at work,
    6. Cracked, chipped or broken window panes positioning of switches, electric or gas in work areas prove a safety hazard. .
    7. Inadequate lighting may produce glare in certain areas and shadows in others affecting visibility and causing injuries.
    8. Improper ventilation, leading to exhaustion and fatigue, makes people vulnerable to accidents.

2. **Accidents From Improper Placement Of Equipment In Spaces** :

1. An electric hot plate placed between two work tables can cause burns
2. Equipment with exposed sharp edges like chopping and slicing machines placed with their sharp edges towards a traffic aisle increases the chances of anyone placing their hand on it accidentally.
3. Mobile equipment like trolleys placed in traffic lanes can cause congestion and collision.
4. Electric switches placed near sinks and on walls behind hot plates, are dangerous arrangements. They can lead people to touch switches with wet hands and suffer shocks
5. Wall cupboards too close to cooking ranges can provide a grave risk of fire.
6. (/) Cooking ranges positioned in a manner that handles of pans placed on them are unsafe.

   Placement of mops, brooms, loosely placed cartons, crates and other packages in traffic areas cause obstruction to work, tripping, falls and consequent injuries.
7. Inadequate provision of and improperly placed fire fighting and other safety equipment, can cause delay in reacting to emergencies.

Accidents From Improper Working Habits:

1. Staff on entering a kitchen lights the gas of cooking ranges, without having anything ready to place on them for cooking can be a potential hazard.
2. Keeping electric switches 'on' while dismantling equipment for cleaning can lead to shocks.
3. Placing knives and other sharp kitchen tools along with other equipment in a sink for washing can cause cuts, because they are not visible to the person doing the washing.
4. Not wiping spillage immediately especially when liquids and hot oils are involved results in dangerous slips and falls.

5. Disposal of broken glass along with the wastes, or postpone complete clearing up of broken debris can cause injuries to those responsible for disposing kitchen wastes and cleaning the equipment or floors.
   (/) Leaving the handles of hot pans ex tending over the edge of the cooking ranges, can cause spillage of hot liquid or oil if people brush past it.
6. Pushing lose wires into electrical sockets when plugs are missing or broken, especially with wet hands can even be fatal.
7. Handling hot bulbs to change them because they have just got fused while working, can bum the hand.
8. Not warning other people of hot electric or gas tops or pans.
9. Lifting lids off pans suddenly and exposing oneself to bums through steam.

a. **Accidents Due To Nature And Behaviour Of People At Work**:

10. Carelessness: It creates conditions unconsciously which are charged with risk.
11. Excitability: Astute of extreme excitement at the slightest provocation puts the mind out of balance, sometimes leading to careless actions are responsible for workers cutting or burning their fingers or spilling oils or hot liquids while working, making floors more slippery and igniting fires .. '
12. Fear: Those who are afraid or hesitant to ask how a job is to be done, for fear of being reprimanded or ridiculed, can adopt unsafe work methods due to ignorance.
13. Anxiety: This can result from some problems outside the work situation; or related to adjustment in a new job or to changed equipment may lead to spillage, slips, and bums.
14. Ill-health: This leads to loss of stamina and easier fatigue; general weakness; poor eyesight and hearing; lowered concentration; and lethargy at work. All these make persons more vulnerable to accidents.

1. Lack of interest in work: Makes people more easily distracted and indifferent to the dangers of handling equipment and other resources in their care.
2. Haste: The man in a hurry is a source of confusion and almost always creates conditions which are unsafe for him and others at work.
3. Lack of concentration: Attention and involvement in the work being done is important especially when working with cutters, slicers or sharp knives and choppers. Very talkative people distract themselves and increase their risk of injury.
4. Forgetfulness: Food and equipment get burnt if placed in an oven and forgotten, the risk of fire is great.

Accidents From Improper Selection, Installation, Maintenance And Storage Of Equipment:

1. Selection of electrical equipment from unrecognized sources or purchase of used equipment; improper earthling may become a source of electrical short circuits or shocks,

   As mentioned earlier sharp unguarded edges in equipment and knives, choppers, etc. are a danger to safety. Leakage from faulty or ill-maintained steam equipment can cause dangerous and painful boils. Even small equipment, like a kitchen knife, need to be kept sharp. More cuts occur from blunt rather than sharp blades.

   Equipment with improper temperature controls or cookers with broken handles are risky to use. Some faults in the design of equipment which makes them unsafe are:

   a. Position of safety valves on equipment. where they are difficult to reach in case of need.
   b. Sinks with taps fitted in positions where water always splashes when used.

Safety Procedure :

1. The controls for all kinds of fuel supplies must be located within easy reach.
2. Spaces where fuel in the form of loaded gas cylinders is stored need to be guarded and isolated from possible sources of ignition and short circuit.
3. Mark all broken or chipped glassware to indicate that they are to be put out of use.
4. Oven pads must be provided for lifting food out of hot ovens or from the top of hot ranges.
5. Regular maintenance procedures must be set up for upkeep of premises and equipment to keep them in safe working order.
6. Every work area should contain aids which remind people of safety, such as posters communicating right and wrong working methods, e.g. "Now wash your hands" written clearly at entrances to kitchens and service areas.
7. Install fire extinguishers and alarms at convenient points in the establishment in case of an emergency.

Safety Training :

SAFETY TECHNOLOGYTECH INNOVATIONS

INTRODUCTION:

Education and training have been recognised as important components of organised health and safety programs in work places. In today's rapidly changing workplace they are more important than ever.

Safety training and education creates consciousness and develops alertness to safety. Safety education develops safety – mindedness while training helps apply acquired safety knowledge to the specific job or task or procedure. It is a process by which employees are helped to develop critical and conscious mind to analyse safe work methods or procedure and develop skills in application of safe methods and practices in their work and activities.

Safety is being implemented by the man on the shop, his conscious efforts to be safe in every situation and at all the times is important. It must be borne in mind that the workers who have not been trained how to perform their jobs safely are more likely to have accidents. It is also a fact that a well-trained employee is more likely to be a safe employee. Therefore, safety consciousness has to be inculcated so that employees' actions and behaviour are all the time governed by such safety considerations.

This article will focus on various aspects of safety training and various statutes applicable to safety training at national and international level, in particular to Indian contest. For the preparation of this article, many documents such as books, articles, acts, rules, codes, and standards are referred, however, due to limitation of space, the list of these references are not included in this article.

SOURCES OF INFORAMTION:

It would be appropriate to go into various aspects of training, such as sources of safety information, designing the training needs, training methods, training plans, so that the readers can get a comprehensive view on safety training.

The objectives of sources of safety information correspond to four different stages of accident sequence.

At the first stage, sources of information provided prior to the task are used to educate workers about risks and persuade them to behave safely. The sources used for this task include safety training materials, hazard communication programmes and various forms of safety programme materials. Methods of education and persuasion attempt not only to reduce errors by improving worker knowledge and skills but also to reduce intentional violation of safety rules by changing unsafe attitudes. As the inexperienced workers are often the target audience at this stage, safety information provided at the stage must be more detailed in content than at other stages.

At the second stage, sources such as written procedures, checklists, instructions, warning signs, and product labels can provide critical safety information during routine task performance. This information usually consists of brief statements, which either instructs less skilled workers or remind skilled workers to take necessary precautions. Statements providing such information are often embedded at the appropriate stage within step-by-step instructions describing how to perform a task. Warning signs at appropriate locations can play a similar role. It must be emphasized that a well-trained and motivated workforce is a prerequisite for safety communication to be effective at this stage.

At the third stage, highly conspicuous and easily perceived sources of safety information alert workers of abnormal or unusually hazardous conditions. The sources of information include warning signals, safety markings, tags, signs, lockouts, etc. As in stage two, a well-trained and motivated workforce is a prerequisite for safety communication to be affective at this stage also.

At the fourth stage, the focus is on expediting worker performance of emergency procedures at the time of an accident, and on the performance of remedial measures shortly after an accident. Safety information signs and markings such as the locations of exists, fire extinguishers, first aid station, emergency showers, eyewash fountains, etc., conspicuously indicate facts critical to adequate performance of emergency procedures. Product safety labels and MSDSs may specify remedial and emergency procedures to be followed. As in stage two and three, a well-trained and motivated workforce is a prerequisite for safety communication to be affective at this stage too.

DESIGNING TRAINING NEEDS:

While designing on the contents of training, the employees' position and the type of work done by him in the organisations need to be considered. The contents must be useful to the trainees' existing work interest and should help him to improve his job performance. In determining the contents, it is profitable to consult, plant or departmental heads and individuals to be trained so as to assess the work interest and areas of work application. This will help in bringing their environment.

It is particularly important to ensure that the key personals that have special safety and health responsibilities within the organisation are properly trained.

Supervisors have a vital role to play in ensuring safety and health. However, often they receive little or no specific training. Therefore, there is a need to train the supervisors in hazard identification and control so that the action can be taken by them to remove hazards from their area of control. It should be borne in mind that safety training should be an integral part of job training and job specification.

New starters to any job are vulnerable and likely to cause / meet accidents and therefore all new starters need to be trained in safety and health relevant to their work before being posted in a position where they are at risk or can become a hazard to others.

Supervisor can ensure that his people are working conscientiously with safe habits, only if he checks from time to time whether the workers know, understand and willingly follow safety rules and regulations. Supervisors shall instil positive attitude to safety, right from the stage of induction training to on-the-job training. General things like use of working space, location of first aid, housekeeping, disposal system, etc., could be stressed in the initial training. While giving details of job instructions, safety points such as use of protective equipment and guards, handling and care of tools, machines, and material and safe methods of working should be emphasized.

To determine the content, it is necessary to have understanding of learning process in view of the trainers' competence and trainees' capacity to learn.

Comprehensive information on company's safety policy, activities and review of company's safety performance in terms of year to year trends, loss of man hours and damage to goods and equipment, etc., can help stressing the role to be played by supervisors and managers for implementation and observance of safety on the shop floor.

TRAINING METHODS:

The training specialists often face within bewildering choice of training methods to meet a defined training objective. It may be borne in mind that what learners retain from instruction they receive vary from person to person. Many educators are of the opinion that the following percentage apply regarding what learners retain from instruction they receive.

- 10 % of what is read
- 20 % of what is heard
- 30 % of what is seen
- 50 % of what is seen and heard
- 70 % of what is seen and spoken
- 90 % of what is said while doing what is talked about

Different training method and techniques are in vogue. The methods, such as lecture, discussion, and role-play technique are useful in a formal classroom for a group of supervisory or management group. The techniques like, on the job instructions, fault analysis are useful for training a small group of technicians or operatives on the shop floor. Project work and simulation workshop help learning through application and practice at any level.

The training method chosen must also maintain interest of the learners. The afternoon sessions must be necessarily conducted by group environment methods so as to keep their interest high, inspite of the odd hours. By and large the methods chosen should help the learners learn the contents through active involvement. All the methods and aids have to be used singly or in combination depending on the type of training, type of trainees, availability of time and facility available for training. The right choice of method or combination of them depends upon the training objective, the learning quality and the speed desired.

TRAINING PLANS:

Before formulating a training plan, it is necessary to clarify some broad aspects of training, such as whether the programme is to meet short term or immediate needs or a long range with future needs in mind. It could also be a general educational programme or the specialised skill development programme. The nature of programme could be induction, orientation for new entrants or refresher, appreciation programme for older employees, etc.

At this stage, it is necessary to find out whether the training content so decided can be taught in a formal training programme or can be put across informally in daily contacts. An informal guidance and coaching can be done individually over a period of time whereas if the group size becomes large, then the formal inputs may be necessary. The induction, orientation, on-the-job programmes have to be organised in the company and can be conducted exclusively by in-company officials.

The duration of the training should however be decided in view of expected results in terms of changes in performance and behaviour and the attempt should be to give adequate coverage so as to reach the expected standard. However, a part-time programme of not more than 2 hours at a time would help keep sustained interest. Programmes organised outside or in institutes have to be full time duration for administrative convenience.

A programme conducted at the premises of the factory has convenience of attending to work and being available when required. However, it suffers from distraction of being called to attend the jobs. Programme away from place of work have an advantage of continuity of learning, minimum interruption, motivation of trainees and adequacy of learning through exchange of views without inhibitions, etc.

The trainers chosen from within the company should be knowledgeable in their subjects and must be interested and skill in teaching. They must be well respected for their position in the organisation and having authority in the subject besides having proven ability to guide and coach people on safety.

The line between training that should be provided by supervisor and health and safety professionals is not clear-cut. Generally speaking, supervisors are more likely to provide job – and task –

specific training while safety and health professionals are more likely to provide the more generic training. Regardless of where this line is drawn, it is clear that today's safety and health professionals must be competent at developing, coordinating and conducting training.

The persons conducting training should have a thorough knowledge of the topics to be taught; a desire to teach; a professional attitude and approach; and exemplary behaviour that sets a positive example. In addition to having these characteristics, the modem trainer should be knowledgeable about the fundamental principles of learning.

STATUTORY REQUIREMENTS:

Having recognised the importance of safety training in workplaces, it would be appropriate to go into various statutory requirements available at National and International Levels.

INDIAN SCENARIO:

Analyses of the causes of accidents, which occurred in India, revealed that the chemical industry accounted for nearly 30 per cent of the fatal accidents and almost the same percentage of nonfatal accidents, which were due to human lapses. These could have been averted if the workers were made aware of the hazards and the preventive control measures and also showed commitment and involvement, which could be achieved through well-planned training programmes. The importance of periodical training, whether formal or informal, has been highlighted by various accidents occurred in India. It must be borne in mind that without the involvement and co-operation of the general public, environmental protection activity in general, and handling of the impact of accidents cannot be very effective. To enlist the involvement and co-operation of the public, an essential requirement is to make them aware of the hazard potentialities. Keeping this requirement in view, the following statutes have provision on training of workers, and some of these have also the stipulation about information to be passed on to the general public:

- The Factories Act 1948.
- The Dock Workers (Safety, Health and Welfare) Regulation 1990.
- The Manufacture, Storage and Import of Hazardous Chemicals (MSIHC) Rules 1989.
- The Central Motor Vehicles (CMV) Rules 1989 as amended in 1993.
- The Mines Act 1952
- The BIS Standards.

Factories Act:

One of the general duties of every 'occupier', prescribed under Section 7A (2) (c), of the Factories Act, 1948, is to provide 'such information, instruction, and training and supervision as are necessary to ensure the health and safety of all workers at work'.

Under Section 41-B of the Factories Act, the occupier of every factory, involving a hazardous process, is to disclose to the workers and the general public, in the prescribed manner, all information regarding the health hazards and the measures to overcome such hazards.

The State Factories Rules framed under the Factories Act have prescribed that the information to be disclosed, shall cover:

1. Requirements of Section 41-B, 41-C and 41-H of the Factories Act.
2. A list of 'hazardous processes' carried on in the factory.
3. Location and availability of all Material Safety Data Sheets.
4. Physical and health hazards arising out of the exposure to or handling of substances.
5. Measures taken by the occupier to ensure safety and control of physical and health hazards.
6. Measures to be taken by the workers to ensure safe handling, storage and transportation of hazardous substances.
7. Personal Protective Equipment required to be used by workers employed in 'hazardous processes or dangerous operation.
8. Meaning of various labels and markings used on the containers of hazardous substances.

Signs and Symptoms likely to be manifested on exposure to hazardous substances and to whom to report.

9. Measures to be taken by the workers in case of any spillage or leakage of hazardous substances.
10. Role of workers vis-à-vis the emergency plan of the factory, in particular the evacuation procedures.
11. Any other information considered necessary by the occupier to ensure safety and health of workers.

The above information shall be compiled and made available to workers individually in the form of booklets or leaflets and display of cautionary notices at the workplace. These will be in the language understood by the majority of the workers. The contents should also be explained to the workers.

Rules under Section 41-B of the Factories Act, also prescribe that every factory carrying on a 'hazardous process' shall obtain or develop information on each hazardous substance handled, maintain it as Material Safety Data Sheets (MSDS), and make these available for reference to the workers, on request.

Section 41-B(1) of the Factories Act prescribes that the occupier of every hazardous process unit shall disclose in the prescribed manner, all information regarding the health hazards in the manufacture, transportation and storage of the hazardous substances, and the measure to combat such hazards, to the general public in the vicinity.

The State Factories Rules prescribe that the occupier of a hazardous process unit shall, in consultation with the designated District Emergency Authority, take appropriate steps to furnish the information to the general public in the area.

Whereas, this is a general requirement applicable to all hazardous process unit, the State Factories Rules have prescribed in the Schedules on dangerous operations, the display of cautionary placards in the following processes specifically:

1. Electrolytic plating (Chromium hazard).

2. Sand blasting.
3. Liming and tanning of raw hides, etc.
4. Manufacture of Chromic Acid.
5. Manufacture of Nitro or Amino processes.
6. Handling and manipulation of corrosive substances.
7. Processes involving the manufacture, use or evolution of Carbon Disulphide and Hydrogen Sulphide.
8. Manufacture & manipulation of dangerous Pesticides.
9. Manufacture & manipulation of Asbestos.
10. Manufacture & manipulation of Manganese
11. Benzene processes.
12. Processes involving carcinogenic dye intermediates
13. Highly flammable liquids and flammable gases.

Dock Workers Regulations:

Training of Dock Workers in the health and safety aspects of cargo handling is as important as the training of workers in the factories. The Dock Workers (Safety, Health and Welfare) Regulations, 1990, cover this aspect also.

Regulation No.111 stipulates that 'initial and periodical training' shall be imparted to all categories of dock workers, responsible and authorised persons depending upon their nature of work and skill required and performing their duties. Training including refresher courses is to be imparted to all first aid personnel, by a qualified medical officer.

MSIHC Rules:

The training provisions in the Manufacture, Storage and Import of Hazardous Chemicals (MSIHC) Rules, 1989, framed under the Environment (Protection) Act, 1986, are meant to equip the workers in the hazardous chemicals units to protect themselves and to avert major accidents in such units, and handle an accident situation appropriately.

Rule 4(2) (b) (ii) of MSIHC Rules, stipulates that the Occupier should 'provide to the persons working on the site with the information, training and equipment including antidotes necessary to ensure their safety'.

Rule 13(4) of MSIHC Rules, prescribes that the Occupier shall ensure that a mock drill of the on-site emergency plan is conducted every six months. This serves as a practical training to the workers on how to handle an accident situation.

Rule 15(1) of MSIHC Rules, stipulates that the Occupier of a hazardous chemical installation shall take all steps to inform the people outside the site either directly or through the District Emergency Authority:(a) the nature of the major accident hazard; and (b) the safety measures and the 'dos' and 'don'ts' to be adopted in the event of a major accident.

Rule 17(1,2,3) of MSIHC Rules, prescribes that the Occupier of a hazardous chemical installation shall maintain Safety Data Sheets (MSDS) on the hazardous chemicals handled and make them accessible to the workers. This stipulation is similar to the one in the Factories Act in respect of hazardous process units.

CMV Rules:

The Central Motor Vehicles Rules, 1989, insists that safety and accident prevention in respect of vehicles transporting hazardous goods are ensured through appropriate information being provided to the drivers who should also be properly trained.

Rule 9(1) of CMV Rules, prescribes that any person driving a goods carriage carrying goods of dangerous or hazardous nature to human life shall: (i) in addition to being the holder of a driving licence to drive a transport vehicle, also has the ability to read and write at least one Indian language out of those specified in the VIII Schedule of the Constitution of India, and English, and (ii) possess a certificate having successfully passed a course consisting of the prescribed syllabus and periodicity (duration – 3 days)

Rule 134 of CMV Rules, stipulates that every goods carriage used for transporting any dangerous or hazardous goods shall be legibly and conspicuously marked with an emergency information panel on three sides of the goods carriage.

Rule 135 of CMV Rules, stipulates that 'the owner' of every goods carriage transporting dangerous or hazardous goods shall ensure that the driver of the goods carriage has received adequate instructions & training to enable him to understand:

- the nature of the goods being transported by him,
- the nature of the risks arising out of such goods,
- the precautions he should take while the goods carriage is in motion or stationary, and
- The action he has to take in case of any emergency.

Mines Act:

The law relating to the regulation of labour and safety in mines in India are governed by Mines Act, 1952.

Rule 58 (ff) of the Mines Act, 1952, insists for training in first-aid; Rule 58 (fff), insists for imparting of practical instruction to, or the training of, persons employed or to be employed in mines; Rule 58 (v) of the Act, provides guidance for the formation, training composition and duties of rescue brigades which are generally for the conduct of rescue work in mines.

BIS Standards:

IS:15001 – 2000 brought out by the Bureau of Indian Standards (BIS), provides guidance to the organizations to develop a practical approach to management of occupational health and safety in such a way to protect employees and general public, whose health and safety may be in danger. The Standard also directs to improve occupational health & safety performance of the organizations by providing the necessary requirements and guidance. However, this standard has been re-designated as IS: 18001-2007.

The BIS has also published National Building Code of India (NBC) 2016, which serves as a guide for all construction activities in India. Part 7 Clause 4.3.9.2 (d) of the NBC 2016 insists for the education and training of workers involved in constructions sites on safety issues. BIS has also published several standards on various aspects of occupational safety, health and environment, which may also serve as a source of information for providing an effective training.

INTERNATIONAL SCENARIO:

In most industrialized countries, government regulations require that certain form of safety information be provided to workers. For example:

In the United States, the Occupational Safety and Health Administration (OSHA) has promulgated a Hazard Communication Standard that applies to workplaces where toxic or hazardous materials are in use, which requires training, container labelling, the distribution of MSDSs and other form of warnings. The Environmental Protection Agency (EPA) has developed several labelling requirements for toxic chemicals. The Department of Transportation (DOT) makes specific provisions regarding the labelling of hazardous materials in transport. It may be noted here that in the U.S., the failure to warn also can be grounds for litigation holding manufacturers, employers and others liable for injuries incurred by workers.

In Canada, the Canadian Centre for Occupational Health and Safety (CCOHS) promotes the total well-being – physical, psychosocial and mental health – of working Canadians by providing information, training, education, management systems and solutions that support health, safety and wellness programs.

In the United Kingdom, the Health and Safety Executive (HSE) is the national regulator for workplace health and safety. It prevents work-related death, injury and ill health. It makes arrangements for and encourages research and publication, training, and information in connection with its work.

In Australia, the Workplace Health and Safety (WHS) laws, previously known as Occupational Health and Safety (OH&S) laws, regulate safety. However, the Safe Work Australia leads the development of national policy to improve work health and safety and workers' compensation arrangements across Australia. Though it does not regulate or enforce WHS legislation, it can however, provide education, training and advice on work health and safety and how to incorporate safety management into the business operations.

A large set of existing standards provides voluntary recommendations regarding the use and design of safety information. These standards have been developed by multilateral groups and agencies, such as the United Nations (UN), the European Economic Community (EEC), the International Labour Office (ILO), the International Organisation for Standardization (ISO) and the International Electro technical Commission (IEC); and by national groups, such as the American National Standards Institute (ANSI), the British Standards Institute (BSI), the Canadian Standards Association (CSA), the German Institute for Normalization (DIN) and the Japanese Industrial Standards Committee (JISC).

It may be remembered here that Occupational Health and Safety (OHS) training is a pre-requisite for obtaining ISO certifications, such as ISO 9001, ISO 14001 and ISO 45001

SAFETY ENGINEERING

Study of the causes and prevention of accidental deaths and injuries. The field of safetyengineering has not developed as a unified, specific discipline, and its practitioners have operated under a wide variety of position titles, job descriptions, responsibilities, and reporting levels in industry and in the loss-prevention activities of insurance companies. The general areas that have been identified as the major functions carried out by the professional safety engineer or safety professional are: the identification and appraisal of accident-producing conditions and practices and the evaluation of the severity of the accident problem; the development of accident and loss-control methods, procedures, and programs; the communication of accident and loss-control information to those directly involved; and the measurement and evaluation of the accident and loss-control systems and the modifications that are required to obtain optimum results.

The most recent trends in safety engineering include increased emphasis on prevention by the anticipation of hazard potentials; changing legal concepts with regard to product liability and negligent design or manufacture, as well as the developing emphasis on consumer protection; and the development of national and international legislation and controls, not only in the areas of transportation safety, product safety, and consumer protection but also in occupational health and environmental control.

SAFETY EDUCATION

Food is a major determinant of health, nutritional status and productivity of the population. It is, therefore, essential that the food we consume is wholesome and safe. Unsafe food can lead to a large number of food borne diseases. You may have seen reports in the newspapers about health problems caused by contaminated or adulterated foods. Globally, food-borne illness is a major problem of public health concern. In India, the National Family Health Survey, 2015 – 2016 stated that more than 9 laky children less than five years of age suffered from acute diarrheal. Food-borne illness can not only result in mortality but can damage trade and tourism, lead to loss of earnings, unemployment and litigation and thus can impede economic growth, and therefore food safety and quality have gained worldwide significance.

Significance Food safety and quality are important at the home level, but are critical in large scale food production and processing, and also where food is freshly prepared and served. In the past, many foods were processed at home. Advancement in technology and processing, higher per capita incomes and better purchasing power as well as increased consumer demand have led to a variety of processed foods, food for health / functional foods being manufactured. Safety of such foods needs to be assessed. The quality of food stuff, raw as well as processed is of public health concern and must be addressed. In the past decade, safety challenges faced globally as well as in India have changed significantly and issues related to food quality and food safety have gained tremendous importance. A number of factors are responsible for this: With fast changing lifestyles and eating habits, more people are eating outside their homes. In commercial settings, foods are prepared in bulk handled by many persons, thus there are more chances of food getting contaminated. Further, food items are prepared many hours in advance, and may spoil if not stored appropriately. There are many processed and packaged foods. Safety of these foods is important. Spices and condiments, oilseeds were processed at home in former times and purity of these were not a concern. In today's world, pre-packaged individual spices, condiments, spice powders and mixes are in demand, especially in cities and metros. Quality of even raw food stuff besides processed foods is of public health concern and must be addressed. Logistics governing transport of bulk food is complex and there is a long gap between processing and consumption. Thus risk assessment and safety management during mass production and mass distribution is critical. Microbial adaptations, antibiotic resistance, altered human susceptibility and international travelling have all contributed to increasing incidence of food-borne microbial diseases. There are still many food borne illnesses of unknown aetiology. This is an issue of global public health concern and there is a need to detect, identify and recognise emerging pathogens and establish active surveillance networks, nationally and internationally. India is a signatory to the World Trade Organisation (WTO) non-tariff agreement, which has provided greater access to world markets and opportunities to all countries to enter international trade. In this scenario, it has become essential for every country to protect the safety and quality of foods and also ensure that imported foods are of good quality and safe to eat. Effective food standards and control systems are required to protect food production within the country as well as to facilitate trade with other nations. All food manufacturers are required to meet the given standards of quality and safety, and need to have their products regularly tested. Pollution in atmosphere, soil and water, including use of pesticides in agriculture, bring their share of contaminants. Also use of additives such as preservatives, colorants, flavouring agents and other substances such as stabilisers makes the analysis of food for various components — both nutrients and contaminants—imperative. Owing to the above factors, there is a growing concern for safe, wholesome and nutritious foods in a highly dynamic food business environment, which in turn has greatly expanded the scope and has increased career opportunities in this sector. Before learning about the various career options in this field, it will be worthwhile for us to understand the basic concepts regarding food quality, food safety, risk assessment, food standards and quality management systems.

II

Introduction to Microbiology in Food Safety

Introduction to microbiology: Relation of microbiology to hygiene – classification of micro – organisms. Factors affecting the growth of micro – organism. Bacteria: Morphology –size, shape structure, reproduction, beneficial and harmful effect of bacteria. Yeast: Morphology – size, shape, structure, reproduction, beneficial and harmful effect of yeast. Meld & classification

Food science is a discipline concerned with all aspects of food - beginning after harvesting, and ending with consumption by the consumer. It is considered one of the agricultural sciences, and it is a field which is entirely distinct from the field of nutrition. The field of food microbiology is a very broad one, encompassing the study of microorganisms which have both beneficial and deleterious effects on the quality and safety of raw and processed foods. It is important to understand the relationships among the various microorganisms making up the microflora of a food. Infact food microbiologists are concerned with the practical implications of the microflora of the food and the food microorganisms that can cause spoilage of food and disease in humans. The primary tool of microbiologists is the ability to identify and quantitative food-borne microorganisms. However, the inherent inaccuracies in enumeration processes, and the natural variation found in all bacterial populations complicate the microbiologist's job. Moreover, they may be important from the aesthetic point of view. Of course, some useful bacteria may be important because they change the functional properties of food stuffs resulting in new tastes, odors or textures. Microorganisms in food include bacteria, molds, yeasts, algae, viruses, parasitic worms and protozoa. These organisms differ in size and shape and in their biochemical and cultural characteristics.

The microorganisms described below are among the most important genera and species normally found in food products. Each microorganism has its own particular nutritional and environmental requirements.

Bacteria

Acinetobacter

Acinetobacter is a genus of Gram-negative bacteria belonging to the Gammaproteobacteria. Acinetobacter species are non-motile and oxidase-negative, and occur in pairs as observed under magnification. Young cultures show rod shaped morphology. They are strict aerobes that do not reduce nitrates. They are important soil and water organisms and are also found on many foods especially refrigerated fresh products. A. baumannii is a frequent cause of nosocomial pneumonia, especially of late onset ventilator associated pneumonia. It can cause various other infections including skin and wound infections, bacteremia, and meningitis,

Bacillus cereus

B. cereus is a thick long rod shaped Gram positive, catalase positive aerobic spore former and the organism is important in food borne illness. It is a normal inhabitant of soil and is isolated from a variety of foods. It is quite often a cause of diarrheal illness due to the consumption of desserts, meat, dishes, dairy products, rice, pasta etc that are cooked and kept at room temperature as it is thermoduric. Some of the B. cereus strains are psychrotrophic as they grow at refrigeration temperature.

B. cereus is spread from soil and grass to cows udders and into the raw milk. It is also capable of establishing in cans. It is also capable of producing proteolytic and amyloltic enzymes and also phoslipase C (lecithinase). The production of these enzymes by these organisms can lead to the spoilage of foods. The diarrheal illness is caused by an enterotoxin produced during the vegetative growth of B. cereus in small intestine. The bacterium has a maximum growth temperature around 48°C to 50°C and pH range 4.9 to 9.3. Like other spores of mesophilic Bacillus species, spores of B. cereus are also resistant to heat and survive pasteurization temperature.

Bacillus Subtilis

Bacillus subtilis , known also as the hay bacillus or grass bacillus , is a Gram-positive, catalase-positive bacterium commonly found in soil. A member of the genus Bacillus, B. subtilis is thin short rod-shaped, and has the ability to form a tough, protective endospore, allowing the organism to tolerate extreme environmental conditions. B. subtilis produces the proteolytic enzyme subtilisin. B. subtilis spores can survive the extreme heat during cooking. B. subtilis is responsible for causing ropiness a sticky, stringy consistency caused by bacterial production of long-chain polysaccharides in spoiled bread dough. A strain of B. subtilis formerly known as Bacillus natto is used in the commercial production of the Japanese food natto, as well as the similar Korean food cheonggukjang. It is used to produce amylase and also used to produce hyaluronic acid, which is useful in the joint-care sector in healthcare.

Carnobacterium

Carnobacterium is a genus of Gram-positive bacteria within the family Leuconostocaceae. C. divergens and C. maltaromaticum are found in the wild and in food products and can grow anaerobically. These species are not known to be pathogenic in humans but may cause disease in fish. The genus Carnobacterium contains nine species, but only C. divergens and C. maltaromaticum are frequently isolated from natural environments and foods. They are tolerant to freezing/thawing and high pressure and able to grow at low temperatures, anaerobically. They metabolize arginine and various carbohydrates, including chitin, and this may improve their survival in the environment. Carnobacterium divergens and C. maltaromaticum have been extensively studied as protective cultures in order to inhibit growth of Listeria monocytogenes in fish and meat products. Several carnobacterial bacteriocins have been identified and described. Carnobacteria can spoil chilled foods, but spoilage activity shows intraspecies and interspecies variation. Their production of tyramine in foods is critical for susceptible individuals, but carnobacteria are not otherwise human pathogens.

Corynebacterium

Corynebacterium is a genus of Gram-positive rod-shaped bacteria. They are widely distributed in nature and are mostly innocuous. Some are useful in industrial settings such as C. glutamicum. Others can cause human disease. C. diphtheriae, for example, is the pathogen responsible for diphtheria. Some species are known for their pathogenic effects in humans and other animals. Perhaps the most notable one is C. diphtheriae, which acquires the capacity to produce diphtheria toxin only after interacting with a bacteriophage. Diphtheria toxin is a single, 60,000 molecular weight protein composed of two peptide chains, fragment A and fragment B, held together by a disulfide bond.

Clostridium perfringens

C. perfringens is a Gram-positive encapsulated anaerobic non-motile bacterium commonly found on meat and meat products. It has the ability to cause food borne disease. It is a toxin producing organism-produces C. perfringens enterotoxin and β -toxin that are active on the human GI tract.

It multiplies very rapidly in food (doubling time < 10 min). Spores are resistant to radiation, desiccation and heat and thus survive in incompletely or inadequately cooked foods.

However, it tolerates moderate exposure to air. Vegetative cells of C. perfringens are also somewhat heat tolerant as they have relatively high growth temperature (43°C -45 °C) and can often grow at 50°C. They are not tolerant to refrigeration and freezing. No growth occurs at 6 °C . C. perfringens is present in soil and the other natural environment.

Clostridium botulinum

C. botulinum produces the most potent toxin known. It is a Gram-positive anaerobic rod shaped bacterium. Oval endospores are formed in stationary phase cultures. There are seven types of C. botulinum (A to G) based on the serological specificity of the neurotoxin produced. Botulism is a rare but very serious disease. The ingestion of neurotoxin produced by the organism in foods can lead to death. However, the toxin (a protein) is easily inactivated by heat. The organism can grow at temperature ranging from 10-48 °C with optimum growth temperature at 37°C. Spores are highly heat resistant. The outgrowth of spores is inhibited at pH < 4.6, NaCl$>$ 10% or water activity$<$ 0.94. Botulinum spores are probably the most radiation resistant spores of public health concern. Contamination of foods is through soil and sediments where they are commonly present. The organism grows under obligate anaerobic conditions and produces toxin in under processed (improper canning) low acid foods at ambient temperature.

Campylobacter

Campylobacter are Gram negative nonspore forming rods. Campyloleacter jejuni is an important food borne pathogen. It is one of the many species within the genus Campylobacter. Campylobacter species C. jejuni and C. coli cause diarrhea in humans. The organism is heat sensitive (destroyed by milk pasteurization temperature). It is also sensitive to freezing. The organism belongs to the family Campylobactereaceae. The organisms are curved, S-shaped, or spiral rods that may form spherical or coccoids forms in old cultures or cultures exposed to air for prolonged periods. Most of the species are microaerophilic. It is oxidase and catalase positive and does not grow in the presence of 3.5% NaCl or at 25 °C or below. The incidence reported for gastro enteritis by this organism is as high as in case of Salmonella.

The organism is commonly present in raw milk, poultry products, fresh meats, pork sausages and ground beef. The infective dose of C.jejuni may be <1,000 organisms.

Erwinia

Erwinia is a genus of the family Enterobacteriaceae bacteria containing mostly plant pathogenic species. The organisms was named after the first phytobacteriologist, Erwin Smith. It is a Gram negative bacterium related to E. coli, Shigella, Salmonella and Yersinia. It is primarily a rod-shaped bacterium. A well-known member of this genus is the species E. amylovora, which causes fire blight on apple, pear and other rosaceous crops. Erwinia carotovora (also known as Pectobacterium carotovorum) is another species, which causes diseases in many plants. These species produce pectolytic enzymes that hydrolyze pectin between individual plant cells. . Decay caused by E. carotovora is often referred to as bacterial soft rot (BSR). Most plants or plant parts can resist invasion by the bacteria, unless some type of wound is present. High humidity and temperatures around 30°C favor development of decay.

Enterococcus (E. faecium, E. faecalis)

Enterococcus is a genus of lactic acid bacteria. Enterococci are Gram positive cocci that often occur in pairs (diplococci) or short chains and are difficult to distinguish from streptococci on physical characters mentioned above. The two species are commensal organisms in the intestine of humans.

The Enterococci are facultative anaerobic organisms non spore forming that grows optimally at 35°C . However, they tolerate wide range of environmental conditions (10-45°C) pH (4.5 to 10.5) quite high NaCl concentration (.6.5%) and can survive heating at 60°C for 30 min.

Catalase-negative, oxidase negative-bacteria of the genes Enterococcus are ubiquitous organisms that often occur in large numbers on vegetables, plant materials and foods especially those of animal origin such as meat and dairy products. Enterococci also constitute a large preparation of autochthonous bacteria associated with the mammalian gastro-intestinal tract.

The resistance of enterococci to pasteurization temperatures and their adaptability to different substrates and growth conditions in food products manufactured from raw materials and in heat treated food products is of great significance.

Enterococci may constitute an important part of the microflora of fermented cheese and meats.

Escherichia coli

E. coli strains are associated with food borne gastroenteritis. These are Gram-negative asprogeneous rods that ferment lactose and produce dark colonies with a metallic sheen on Endo agar. The organism grows well on a large number of media and in many foods. They grow over a wide range of temperature (4 to 46 °C) and pH (4.4 to 9.0).

However, they grow very slowly in foods held at refrigerator temp. (5 °C). They belong to the family Enterobacteriaceae. The organism is also an indicator of fecal pollution. The organism is also capable of producing acid and gas and off-flavours in foods. E. coli strains involved in foodborne-illness can be placed into five groups: enteropathogenic (EPEC), enterotoxigenic (ETEC), enteroinvasive (EIEC), enterohemorrhagic (EHEC) and facultatively enteropathogenic (FEEC).

The organism also grows in the presence of bile salts. The primary habitat of E.coli is the intestinal tract of most warm blooded animals. E.coli 0157: H7 strains are unusually tolerant of acidic environments.

Lactococcus

Lactococcus is a genus of lactic acid bacteria that were formerly included in the genus Streptococcus Group N (Group N Streptococci). They are known as homofermentors meaning that they produce a single product of glucose fermentation. They are Gram-positive, catalase negative, non-motile coccus that are found singly, in pairs or in chains. Some of the strains of lactococci are known to grow at or below 7 °C.

Lactococci are intimately associated with dairy products. These organisms are commonly used in the dairy industry in the manufacture of fermented dairy products like cheeses. They can be used in single strain starter cultures or in mixed strain cultures with other lactic acid bacteria such as Lactobacillus and Streptococcus. Their main purpose in dairy production is the rapid acidification of milk. This causes drop in the pH of fermented product which prevents the growth of spoilage and pathogenic bacteria. These bacteria also play a role in the flavor of the final product. Dairy lactococci have also been exploited for several industrial fermentations in the biotechnology industry. They are easily grown at industrial scale up on cheap whey based media.

Lactococcus lactis subsp. lactis includes species formerly designated as S. lactis subsp. lactis. L. lactis subsp. cremoris is distinguished from L. Lactis subsp. lactis by the inability to (i) grow at 40 °C (ii) grow in 4% NaCl (iii) hydrolyse arginine and (iv) ferment ribose.

Lactococcus

The organisms belonging to this important genus are rods usually long and slender and in some of the species form chains. They are aerotolerant/microaerophilic but some ferment sugars chiefly to lactic acids if they are homofermentative. The hetero fermentative species, besides lactic acid, also produce small amount of acetic acid, carbon dioxide and trace amounts of volatile compounds such acetaldehyde and alcohol. The homofermentative species of Lactobacillus include L. bulgaricus, L. casei, L. helveticus, L. lactis, L. acidophilus and grow optimally at 37 °C. L. fermentum, L. brevis are the typical example of hetero fermentative Lactobacillus and grow well at higher temperatures.

Lactobacilli are of considerable importance in foods as they ferment sugar to lactic acid and other desirable flavouring compounds and are thus used in the production of fermented plant dairy and meat products. However, they are also implicated in the spoilage of wine and beer.

The organism normally occurs on plant surfaces silage, manure and dairy products. They are quite fastidious in their nutritional requirements as they are unable to synthesize certain vitamins they require and, therefore, media need to be supplemented with these vitamins for their growth.

Some of the strains are psychotrophic in nature and are thus involved in the spoilage of refrigerated meats. On the other hand thermoduric properties (resistance to pasteurization temperature) of some of the thermophilic strains of lactobacilli are quite useful in the manufacture of certain varieties of cheeses e.g. Swiss cheese. Some strains of lactobacilli also show probiotic attributes and are finding application in functional probiotic foods and in pharmaceutical preparations.

Leuconostoc

Leuconostoc is a genus of Gram-positive bacteria, placed within the family of Leuconostocaceae. They are generally ovoid cocci often forming chains. Leuconostoc spp. are intrinsically resistant to vancomycin and are catalase-negative (which distinguishes them from staphylococci). All species within this genus are heterofermentative and are able to produce dextran from sucrose. They are generally slime-forming. Blamed for causing the 'stink' when creating a sourdough starter, some species are also capable of causing human infection.

Leuconostoc spp. along with other lactic acid bacteria such as Pediococcus and Lactobacillus spp , is responsible for the fermentation of cabbage, to sauerkraut. In this process the sugars in fresh cabbage are transformed to lactic acid which give it a sour flavour and good keeping qualities.

Listeria monocytogenes

Listeria monocytogenes in foods has attracted worldwide attention due to the serious illness it causes in human beings. The Listeria are Gram positive non spore forming, nonacid-fast rods. The organism is catalase positive and produces lactic acid from glucose and other fermentable sugars. The organism grows well in brain heart infusion (BHI), trypticase soy, and tryptose broths. However, the medium should be fortified with B. vitamins and the amino acids. It is a mesophilic organism with optimal growth temperature 37°C but it can grow at refrigerator temperature also.

Strains grows over the temperature range of 1°C to 45°C and pH range 4.1 to 9.6.

Listeria monocytogenes is widely distributed in nature and can be isolated from decaying vegetation, soil, animal feces, sewage, silage and water. The organism has been found in raw milk, pork, raw poultry, ground beef and vegetables. The HTST treatment of pasteurization is good enough to destroy the organism in milk.

The most significant virulence factor associated with L. monocytogenes is listeriolysin O. The virulent strains produce β-hemolysis on blood agar and acid from rhamnose.

L. monocytogenes grows well in moderate salt concentrations (6.5%).

L. monocytogenes is unique among foodborne pathogens while other pathogens excrete toxins or multiply in the blood stream, L. monocytogenes enters the host's cells and grows inside the cell. In humans it crosses the intestinal barrier after entering by the oral route.

Ready to Eat (RTE) foods that are preserved by refrigeration pose a special challenge with regard to L. monocytogenes infection.

Micrococcus

Micrococcus occurs in a wide range of environments, including water, dust, and soil. Micrococci are Gram-positive spherical cells ranging from about 0.5 to 3 micrometers in diameter and typically appear in tetrads. Micrococcus has a substantial cell wall, which may comprise as much as 50% of the cell mass. Some species of Micrococcus, such as M. luteusM. roseus (red) produce yellow or pink colonies when grown on mannitol salt agar. Micrococcus is generally thought to be a saprophytic or commensal organism, though it can be an opportunistic pathogen, particularly in hosts with compromised immune systems, such as HIV patients.

Proteus

Since it belongs to the family of Enterobacteriaceae, general characters are applied on this genus: It is oxidase-negative, but catalase and nitrate reductase positive. Three species P. vulgaris, P. mirabilis, and P. penneri are opportunistic human pathogens.

Proteus includes pathogens responsible for many human urinary tract infections. P. mirabilis causes wound and urinary tract infections. Most strains of P. mirabilis are sensitive to ampicillin and cephalosporins. P. vulgaris is not sensitive to these antibiotics. However, this organism is isolated less often in the laboratory and usually only targets immune suppressed individuals. P. vulgaris occurs naturally in the intestines of humans and a wide variety of animals; also manure, soil and polluted waters. P. mirabilis, once attached to urinary tract, infects the kidney more commonly than E. coli. P. mirabilis are often found as free-living organisms in soil and water.

Propionibacterium spp. (P. freudenreichii)

Historically, Propionibacterium spp. are of interest because of their use as dairy starters (especially in the production of Swiss-type cheese) and their ability to produce propionic acid during growth. The genus Propionibacterium is generally split into "cutaneous" and "dairy" groups. The dairy Propionibacterium spp. can also be isolated primarily from dairy foods and silage. The species in dairy products include P. jensenii, P. acidipropionici, P. theoniiP. freudenreichii. Propionibacteria have a role in the production of flavour compounds in cheese by proteolysis and propionic acid production. Dairy strains of propionibacteria are autolytic under environmental conditions found in cheese and degrade peptides and amino acids that are present in the cheese. and

The dairy species offer an interesting opportunity as novel probiotic organisms with the most obvious advantage being that they are considered safe for ingestion.

Propionibacterium

Pediococci compromise a group of bacteria that are of economic importance in the brewing and food industries. Several species and strains of pediococci have been used as starter cultures in the fermentation of vegetables, meats, sausage products, fermented milks and associated with the development of flavor in Cheddar and other related cheese varieties. Some strains form capsular material that causes beer to become ropy and viscous.

They are catalase negative and exhibit a homolactic type of fermentation and produce optically inactive lactic acid i.e. a mixture of the L(+) and D(-) type. They generally appear in tetrads.

Pseudomonas fluorescens

Pseudomonas fluorescens is a common Gram-negative, rod-shaped, motile bacterium. The organism is psychrotrophic in nature and grows at refrigeration temperature (7°C). It has an extremely versatile metabolism, and can be found in the soil and in water. It is an obligate aerobe, but certain strains are capable of using nitrate instead of oxygen as a final electron acceptor during cellular respiration. Optimal temperature for growth of Pseudomonas fluorescens is 25-30 °C. It tests positive for the oxidase. Pseudomonas fluorescens is also a nonsaccharolytic organism. Heat-stable lipases and proteases are produced by Pseudomonas fluorescens and other similar pseudomonads. These enzymes cause milk to spoil, by causing bitterness, casein breakdown, and ropiness due to the production of slime and coagulation of proteins.

Pseudomans aeruginosa

It is a Gram-negative, aerobic, rod-shaped bacterium with unipolar motility. An opportunistic human pathogen, P. aeruginosa is also an opportunistic pathogen of plants. P. aeruginosa is the type species of the genus Pseudomonas (Migula). Gram-stained Pseudomonas aeruginosa bacteria (pink-red rods) secretes a variety of pigments, including pyocyanin (blue-green), pyoverdine (yellow-green and fluorescent), and pyorubin (red-brown). P. aeruginosa is often preliminarily identified by its fluroscence and grape-like or tortilla-like odor in vitro. Definitive clinical identification of P. aeruginosa often includes identifying the production of pyocyanin and fluorescein, as well as its ability to grow at 42°C. P. aeruginosa is capable of growth in diesel and jet fuel, where it is known as a hydrocarbon-using microorganism (or "HUM bug"), causing microbial corrosion. P. aeruginosa is considered by many as a facultative anaerobe

Pseudomonas aeruginosa

Salmonella (S. typhimurium, S. typhi, S.enteritidis)

Salmonella spp. have been reported to be a leading cause of foodborne illnesses in humans. Foodborne salmonellosis scores over all other foodborne bacterial illnesses in humans. Enteric fever is a serious human disease associated with typhoid and paratyphoid strains. SalmonellaEnterobacteriaceae. The optimum growth temperature is 37-45 °C. The organism can also grow at about 7°C in foods. I t ferments carbohydrates with its production of acid and gas. Salmonella are oxidase negative, catalase positive and grow on citrate as a sole carbon source and produce H2S. Some Salmonella strains can grow at higher temperatures (54 °C) while others exhibit psychrotrophic properties. The organism has the ability to grow at pH values ranging from 4.5 to 9.5, with an optimum pH growth at 6.5 to 7.5. spp. are facultatively anaerobic, small Gram-negative, non spore forming, rod-shaped (2-4 m m) bacteria belonging to the family

Milk, meat and poultry are principle vehicles of human foodborne salmonellosis. Ingestion of only a few salmonella cells can be infectious. Low levels of salmonellae in a finished food products may, therefore, be of serious public health consequence.

Salmonella

Serratia

Serratia is a genus of Gram-negative, facultatively anaerobic, rod-shaped bacteria of the Enterobacteriaceae family. The most common species in the genus, S. marcescens, is normally the only pathogen and usually causes nosocomial infections. However, rare strains of S. plymuthica, S. liquefaciens, S. rubidaea, and S. odoriferae have caused diseases through infection. Members of this genus produce characteristic red pigment, prodigiosin.

Streptococcus thermophilus

The only streptococcus species that is associated with food technology is S. thermophilus which is used in the manufacture of yoghurt (in co culture with L. bulgaricus and Dahi).

S. thermophilus is a Gram positive facultative anaerobe and belongs to the family Streptococcaceae. It is catalase negative organism that is non-motile, non-spore forming and homofermentative and occurs in pairs to long chains. The spherical to avoid cells are with a diameter in the range of 0.7 to 0.9 μm. The optimum temperature for the growth of this organism is between 39°C to 45°C, although most species in the genus are able to grow at temperature ranging from 45-60°C. They do not grow at temperature below 20°C, but they can survive at 65°C for 30 min. They ferment sugars with L (+) lactic acid as the major end product and produce around 0.6 to 0.8% lactic acid. They are able to grow in broth with 2.5% NaCl but fail to grow in 6.5% NaCl at pH 9.6 or in milk with 0.1% methylene blue (Bergey's Manual 1994). It is also classified as lactic acid bacteria (LAB). It is a very versatile organism. S. thermophilus has properties that make it one of the commercially most important lactic acid organism. S. thermophilus is used along with Lactobacillus spp., as a starter culture to manufacture several important fermented dairy foods including yoghurt and moarella cheese.

Though the natural habitat of S. thermophilus is yet to be established, most strains have been isolated from milk environments.

Streptococcus thermophilus

Staphylococcus aureus

Staphylococcus aureus is commonly associated with humans. It is a Gram-positive catalase-positive coccus. Staphylococcus aureus is the common cause of foodborne gastroenteritis known as staphylococcal food poisoning. Staphylococcal gastroenteritis is caused by the ingestion of food that contains one or more enterotoxin which are produced by some strains of S. aureus.

Although enterotoxin production is believed generally to be associated with coagulase and thermo nuclease producing S. aureus strains, many species of Staphylococcus that produce neither coagulase nor TNase are also known to produce enterotoxin.

The main reservoir of S. aureus is the nasal cavity of human beings from where they find their way to the skin and wounds. Mastitis in animals due to S. aureus is quite common and from the infected udder the organism finds its way to the milk.

The organism can grow well in NaCl concentrations of 7 to 10%. Though the optimum growth temperature of the organism is 37 °C , some strains can grow at a temperature as low as 6.7 °C. The organism can grow to water activity as low as 0.86.

Staphylococcus

Shigella

Bacillary dysentery, or shigellosis, is caused by Shigella species. Shigella is a member of the family Enterobacteriaceae. The growth temperature varies from 10 to 48 °C. Shigella2S. Shigella does not usually survive well in low pH foods. Shigella is sensitive to ionizing radiations. species are non-motile, oxidase negative produce acid only from sugars; do not grow on citrate as sole carbon source, do not grow on KCN agar, and unlike Salmonellae do not produce H

Shigellosis is an important disease in developed and developing countries. Disease is caused by ingestion of contaminated foods, and in some instances it subsequently leads to rapid dissemination through contaminated feces from infected individuals. The infective dose may be as low as 100 cells. Contamination of foods usually does not occur at the processing plant but rather through an infected food handler. Humans are the natural reservoir of Shigella. The organism is spread through the fecal-oral route.

Vibrio

Vibrio cholerae and V. parahaemolyticus are the two important species of the genus Vibrio. Vibrio cholerae O1 causes cholera, one of the few food borne illnesses with epidemic and pandemic potential. Vibrio cholerae are Gram-negative straight or curved rods and belong to the family Vibrionaceae. Important distinctions within the species are made on the basis of productions of cholera enterotoxin (CT) and serogroup.

Vibrio cholerae is part of the normal free living bacterial flora in estuarine areas. Amongst the many different enrichment broths described for the isolation of vibrios alkaline peptone water is the most commonly used. Though V. parahaemolyticus can grow in the presence of 1-8% NaCl, the best growth occurs in the salt concentration 2 to 4%.

Yersinia

Yersinia enterocolitica and Yersinia pestis are the two important human pathogens while Y. enterocolitica causes food borne gastroenteritis, Y. pestis is an agent of human plague. Y. enterocolitica also known as newly emerging human pathogen is a heterogeneous species that is divisible into a large number of subgroups.

Y. enterocolitica is unusual because it can grow at temperatures below 4 °C. The generations time at the 28-30 °C (Optimum growth temperature) is almost 34 min. It also survives in frozen foods. It grows better in processed foods such as pasteurized milk, vacuum packed meat, boiled eggs, boiled fish, and cottage cheese.

Both the species can grow over a pH range of 4 to 10 (optimum pH is 7.6) and tolerate alkaline environment well. They can motile at a temperature < 30 °C. However, both these organisms are susceptible to pasteurization, ionizing and ultraviolet (UV) irradiation. The organism can also tolerate upto 5% NaCl.

Infections with Yersinia species are due to transmittance of the organism from animals to humans. The organism is frequently present in pork, lamb, poultry and dairy products.

Relation of microbiology to hygiene

The domestic/household kitchen has always been associated with food preparation, and largely extends to both consumption and storage. A typical kitchen comprises of various gadgets and appliances, ranging from small items such as spoons, knives and cutting boards to large appliances such as microwave ovens, dishwashers and cookers. And potentially, how complete a kitchen typically is would largely depend on the household's economic status. Regardless of how equipped a typical household kitchen may appear to be, it is most likely that the level of food safety awareness, knowledge and practice of a given kitchen user might directly associate with the hygiene situation of a given kitchen. Besides, there are some basic food hygiene/ microbiological safety (FHMS) concept definitions that all kitchen users should possess. By having so, they (kitchen users) will become equipped with some useful knowledge base to help build-up their capacity to actualize, realize and sustain a healthy kitchen environment. Keeping the components of household kitchen at top-notch hygiene condition is very essential because such practice would help consolidate kitchen users' efforts in implementing the microbiological safety at all food preparation/storage stages. And by achieving such feat, the microbiological safety of a food dished out from a (typical) household kitchen can be considered as consumer protected and safe. Clearly, consumers are very useful candidates within their kitchen environment contexts given their capacity to prevent the incidence as well as spread of foodborne diseases/illnesses.

The primary purpose of food hygiene is to eliminate or reduce the risk of (human) exposure to foodborne illness. This, and with respect to household kitchen environment, can be achieved when kitchen users have acquired some thorough knowledge and understanding of kitchen components and its associated microbial hygiene/safety, coupled with some basic principles of food hygiene /microbiological safety. Therefore, activities within the kitchen should be such that adhere to good food safety attitudes and practices. For example, Hazard Analysis and Critical Control Points (HACCP) recognized by Food and Agricultural Organization (FAO) of the United Nations, European Commission, Australian and New Zealand Food Authority and World Health Organization (WHO) are already becoming increasingly popular in developing countries as a tool that ensures food safety1. Although many consumers have often expressed concern about restaurant kitchens and public dining places, there is evidence of statistics that show a significant number of all foodborne outbreaks actually occur in homes. According to the most current Centre for Disease Control (CDC) surveillance report, in 2016 alone, there were 76 outbreaks (10%) and 895 reported cases of illness (7%) in the United States, which were attributed to food prepared in private homes2. On the other hand, the European Food Safety Authority (EFSA) indicated the most reported setting for foodborne disease outbreaks were registered as 'household/domestic kitchen'

Whilst home kitchens are well known to serve, not only as storage place(s), but also as multipurpose areas, consumers have a critical key role to play in the prevention of foodborne disease incidence. Besides, the different sources from which microorganisms can be transferred to food are well known. These include: the hands, body fluids or clothing worn by individual preparing the food; unclean kitchen utensils, unclean water for cooking, house pets, etc. Any living or non-living thing found in the kitchen, which may harbor microorganisms that can be transferred to food at any stage of preparation, may serve as a source of contamination. Indeed, contamination of food by microorganisms can occur in any of several stages of food preparation, from raw food and ingredients, the cooking or preparation process up to handling and storage of the cooked food.

- Contamination of raw food and ingredients: Many raw foods including vegetables, tubers, roots, which are grown in the soil, are naturally contaminated by microorganisms in the soil and even after washing, cells of such microorganisms remain on the raw food. Fruits on trees contain deposits of microbial cells and spores from the air. Raw foods from animal sources, such as meats and milk are contaminated with microorganisms from the animals' skin and intestines during slaughter and milking, respectively.
- Contamination during cooking: Contamination during cooking occurs when microorganisms introduced into the food as described above or introduced from unclean water used for cooking, unclean cooking utensils, hands, sneeze, cough or other body secretions, are not eliminated during the cooking process. Most bacteria associated with foodborne illness will be killed if exposed to temperatures between 60 and 80°C; mold fungi will require higher temperatures, while both bacterial and fungal spores will require temperatures near boiling or higher. If the food containing these microbial elements is not cooked such that every part of the food attains the appropriate temperature,

the contaminants may remain in the food. Moreover, vegetables usually are not heated to high temperature. Therefore, the contaminating microorganisms must be eliminated by mechanisms other than heat.

- Contamination of cooked food: The most common mechanism of contamination of cooked food is the improper handling of the ready-to-eat food, which allows microorganisms from raw food or unclean objects to touch the ready-to-eat food. For example, while frying chicken, the kitchen user may use the same spatula to go from the raw chicken to the already fried chicken, transferring microbes to the ready-to-eat chicken in the process.

In the light of the abovementioned information (and others not mentioned) that may be found in the typical household kitchen, there is need to examine its food hygiene/microbiological safety (FHMS) aspects, in the view to supplement existing information. Therefore, the specific objective of this contribution is to perform a concise review about food hygiene and microbiological safety in the typical household kitchen. Here, we break down this important food-health household topic into fundamental and simpler phases/points, with the aim to make contents of the evolving sub-topics bit less technical, with increasing clarity and understanding for the average home kitchen user as well as wider scientific community. This concise review is constructed as follows: some basic food hygiene /microbiological safety (FHMS) concept definitions applicable to domestic/household kitchen; snapshots of some key foodborne pathogens and corresponding diseases/illnesses; kitchen components and associated microbial hygiene/safety; food hygiene and microbiological safety in a typical kitchen; as well as human activities/participation in food hygiene microbiological safety.

Some Basic Food Hygiene/Microbiological Safety (FHMS) Concept Definitions Applicable to Domestic/Household Kitchen

To achieve high level of food hygiene/microbiological safety in the typical domestic/household kitchen should, in our opinion, start with acquisition of both knowledge and understanding of some fundamental concept definitions and associated endeavor(s). Such knowledge and understanding would help shed more light about the principles underscoring food hygiene microbiological safety contexts and feasibly any (associated/relevant) applications. Herein, some basic food hygiene/microbiological safety concepts associated with kitchen, according to the discretion of authors are succinctly highlighted below: cross-contamination, susceptibility, food hygiene/safety/poisoning, foodborne disease/illnesses, safe handling practices, disinfecting/disinfectant, cleaning/sanitizing, microbial growth/proliferation, reservoir of foodborne illness, dissemination of foodborne disease, resident microbial flora, microbial biofilms, signs/symptoms, nausea, bacteremia, septicemia, diarrhea, hemorrhage and pathogenicity/virulence. These concept definitions below are succinctly outlined:

Cross-contamination

According to United States Department of Agriculture (USDA), cross-contamination is the transfer of harmful bacteria to food from other foods, cutting boards, utensils, etc., if they are not handled properly. This is especially true when handling raw meat, poultry, and seafood, so keep these foods and their juices away from already cooked or ready-to-eat foods and fresh produce4.

Susceptibility with respect to food safety

This is the capability of an individual to get sick from contaminated food. For example, vulnerable people such as the very aged/elderly or ill/sick are more susceptible to infection caused by foodborne pathogens that would result in serious consequences compared to healthy adults5.

Food hygiene

According to World Health Organization (WHO), food hygiene refers to the conditions and measures necessary to ensure the safety of food from production to consumption. Food can become contaminated at any point during slaughtering or harvesting, processing, storage, distribution, transportation and preparation. Lack of adequate food hygiene can lead to foodborne diseases and death of the consumer6.

Food safety

According to Australian Institute of Food Safety, food safety refers to the handling, preparing and storing food in a way to best reduce the risk of individuals becoming sick from foodborne illnesses. Food safety is a global concern that covers a variety of different areas of everyday life

Food poisoning

According to Better Health Channel of Victoria State Government of Australia, food poisoning occurs when sufficient numbers of particular types of bacteria, or their toxins, are present in the food we consume. It is these bacteria that are termed 'pathogens' Foodborne disease

According to WHO, foodborne diseases are understood to encompass a wide spectrum of illnesses, which result from ingestion of foodstuffs contaminated with either chemicals or microorganisms. Importantly, the contamination of food may occur at any stage, from food production to consumption, and can emerge from environmental contamination, including pollution of water, soil or air

Foodborne illnesses

According to National Institute of Diabetes and Digestive and Kidney Diseases (NIDDK), foodborne illnesses are understood as infections or irritations of the gastrointestinal (GI) tract caused by food or beverages that contain harmful bacteria, parasites, viruses, or chemicals. The GI tract is a series of hollow organs joined in a long, twisting tube from the mouth to the anus. Common symptoms of foodborne illnesses include vomiting, diarrhea, abdominal pain, fever, and chills

Safe handling practice in food safety

This concept is well to known and largely describes guidelines/ processes by which potential hazards/risks in food products are minimized, with the aim to enhance both productivity and quality.

Disinfectant

According to the Center for Disease Control and Prevention (CDC), the term 'disinfectant' is ascribed to chemical agent(s) used on inanimate objects (i.e., nonliving) (e.g., floors, walls, sinks) to destroy virtually all recognized pathogenic microorganisms, but not necessarily all microbial forms (e.g., bacterial endospores). The EPA has grouped disinfectants based on whether the product label claims/indicates "limited," "general" or "hospital" disinfectant

Disinfection

According to the Center for Disease Control and Prevention (CDC), the term 'disinfection' refers to the destruction of pathogenic and other kinds of microorganisms by physical or chemical means. Disinfection is less lethal than sterilization, because it destroys most recognized pathogenic microorganisms, but not necessarily all microbial forms, such as bacterial spores. Disinfection does not ensure the margin of safety associated with sterilization processes

Cleaning

According tocleaning removes food and other types of soil from a surface such as a countertop or plate

Sanitizing

According to sanitizing reduces the number of pathogens on that clean(ed) surface to safe levels

Microbial growth

In microbiology, the concept 'microbial growth' is defined as a process of increase in the number of cells of an organism. For example, bacteria grow and divide by binary fission, a rapid and relatively simple process. Fundamentally, requirements for growth are physical (temperature, pH, osmotic pressure) and chemical (from carbon, nitrogen, sulphur, phosphorus, up to oxygen)

Microbial proliferation.This simply refers to continuous increase in microbial growth/numbers, which to a large extent depends on organism(s) type present as well as initial concentration of microorganisms

Reservoir of foodborne illness.According to Victoria State of Government of Australia's hub for health services, whilst soil, dust, cereals serve as reservoirs for food and water-borne illness, and fish, birds, reptiles, and wild and domestic mammals serve as reservoirs for bacteria and parasites, humans serve as the reservoir for viruses

Dissemination of foodborne disease/illness.This well-known term widely considers the ability of a vector to distribute a microbial pathogen between one location and another location.

Resident microbial flora

According to WHO Guidelines on Hand Hygiene in Healthcare, the resident flora (resident microbiota) are understood to consist of microorganisms residing under the superficial cells of the stratum corneum and can also be found on the surface of the skin.

Microbial biofilms

complex communities of microorganisms attached to surfaces or associated with interfaces. Such microbial communities are often composed of multiple species that interact with each other and their environment. The determination of biofilm architecture particularly the spatial arrangement of micro-colonies (clusters of cells) relative to one another have profound implications for the function of these complex communities.

Signs and symptoms

These (signs and symptoms) are abnormalities indicative of potential ill-health/medical conditions. Whereas a symptom is subjective, that is, apparent only to the patient (for example, back pain and or fatigue), a sign is any objective evidence of an emergent disease condition, detected/observed by others (for example, a skin rash or lump).

Nausea

This is a stomach discomfort resulting in sensation of want to vomit. It can be an originator to vomiting the contents of the stomach, and such condition has many causes and can often be prevented.

Bacteremia

This is an infection caused by bacteria that enters the bloodstream. It may also be referred to either as septicemia, sepsis, septic shock, blood poisoning and/or bacteria in the blood.

Septicemia

Sepsis and septicemia are medical terms that refer to infections and human body response to such infections. Whilst the two words are not interchangeable (as it appears to be commonly so), sepsis is an extreme inflammatory response to infection, whereas septicemia is presence of bacteria in bloodstream that brings about sepsis, hence 'blood poisoning'.

Diarrhea

A common health complaint characterized by abnormally loose/ watery stool, largely caused either by bacteria, virus and/or parasites, which brings about infection in gastrointestinal tract. Examples of bacteria that would cause diarrhea include Hemorrhage.It can refer either to blood loss inside (internal bleeding) or outside (external bleeding) the body, and can occur in almost any area of the body.

Pathogenicity

This term refers to the ability of an organism to cause disease (i.e., harm the host). This ability represents a genetic aspect of pathogen together with overt damage done to the host as property of host-pathogen interactions.

Virulence

This is a term often used interchangeably with pathogenicity. It refers to the degree of pathology caused by a given organism. The extent of virulence actually correlates with pathogen's ability to multiply within the host and may be affected by other factors, i.e., conditional.For a re-emphasis, the reason that we provide these concept definitions is to present readers with necessary background knowledge so as to understand the relevant food hygiene microbiological safety contents as well as contexts, whenever or wherever there are mentioned. This will place readers to be in a better position particularly those who are non-microbiology experts to adequately follow subsequent sections reasonably better, starting with some key foodborne pathogens and its corresponding diseases/illnesses.Snapshots of Some Key Foodborne Pathogens and Corresponding Diseases/Illnesses. Having dealt with some food hygiene/microbiology safety concept definitions, we will in this section provide snapshots of some key foodborne pathogens, particularly such bacteria as and their corresponding diseases/illnesses. To elaborate on these, the emphasis will be given to reservoir animals associated with these pathogens, food vehicles, mode of transmission and how disease in human eventually manifests via signs/symptoms. How such disease are treated will neither be highlighted nor discussed in this section (and current work) because authors deem it not within the remit of the specific objective of this concise review. We aim here to emphasize on foodborne pathogens and corresponding diseases/ illnesses potentially foreseeable in the typical household kitchen context so kitchen users to be aware that such foodborne pathogens do exist and can find its way into the kitchen particularly if hygiene standards get compromised to very low levels. And as such, all should be carried out in such a way to ensure high hygiene standards are maintained so as to prevent any disease incidence.

1) Salmonella bacteria (with Salmonella typhimurium involved as principal species) have poultry, bovine, ovine, porcine and fish/ seafood as reservoir animals. Hence, food vehicles can include poultry meat products, and eggs, undercooked meat or ground beef, as well as dairy products. The mode of transmission is ingestion of food or contaminated water, consumption of food of infected animal products. The disease in humans is largely localized gastroenteritis with such principal signs/symptoms as nausea, vomiting, diarrhea, bacteremia, and up to septicemia25. Factors determining the virulence of Salmonella genus bacteria that allows for its infection and survival involves mechanisms of adherence to host's cells, invasion and replication inside host's cells, polysaccharide coating, and up to the production of toxins.

2) Campylobacter bacteria (with Campylobacter coli and C. jejuni as involved principal species) have poultry, cattle, pigs and piglets as reservoir animals. Thus, food vehicles can include poultry products, unpasteurized milk and water. The mode of transmission includes ingestion of contaminated food or water as well as consumption of food infected animals. The disease in human is Campylobacteriosis with such principal signs/symptoms as acute diarrhea, abdominal pain, fever, intestinal bloody diarrhea, oesophageal diseases,

functional gastrointestinal disorders, celiac disease, and up to colon cancer25. The attribute of Campylobacter genus bacteria that allows for its infection and survival involves mechanisms of mobility, drug resistance, adherence to host's epithelial cells, invasion of host's cells and production of toxins.

3) Listeria bacteria (with Listeria monocytogenes as involved principal species) have cattle, sheep, goats and poultry as reservoir animals. Thus, food vehicles can include crustaceans, mollusks, shellfish, cheese, beef, pork, vegetables and milk products. The mode of infection involves ingestion of contaminated food or water, direct content with infected animals or consumption of food from infected animals and person-to-person contact. The disease in human is Listeriosis with such principal signs/symptoms as invasive illness like meningitis, bacteremia, endocarditic, and up to non-invasive illness like febrile gastroenteritis. In addition, factors that determine the pathogenicity of L. monocytogenes that substantiates its virulence involve adhesive protein, listeriolysin O, secretion systems, phospholipases C (PlcA and PlcB), superficial proteins ActaA, and the OrfX protein.

4) Yersinia bacteria (with Yersinia enterocolitica as involved principal species) have cattle, sheep and pig as reservoir animals. Thus food vehicles can include raw or undercooked pork, but also fresh and pasteurized milk, infected seafood as well as (drinking) water. The mode of infection involves ingestion of contaminated food or water, direct contact with infected animals, infected tissues and person-to-person contact. The disease in human is yersinosis with such principal signs/symptoms as severe gastritis and enteritis, fever, stomachache, diarrhea (often bloody) with complications like erythema, myocarditis, and less often sepsis and endocarditis. Besides, factors/mechanisms that facilitates the infection of Y. enterocolitica involves adhesion and invasion of host's cells, secretion system type III mobility, lipopolysaccharides, thermo-stable enterotoxins, production of urease, and up to avoidance of host's immunological response.

5) Shiga toxin-producing Escherichia coli bacteria (with Senogroup O151 as most common but O26, O45, O103, O111, O121 and O145 as involved principal species) has cattle, sheep, goats and a lower proportion of pigs, cats and (some) other ruminants. Hence, food vehicles can include undercooked ground meat, raw milk, raw vegetables, fruits, water, cheese and curd. The mode of transmission involves ingestion of contaminated food or water, direct contact with infected animals or consumption of food from infected animals and person-to-person contact. The disease in human is severe hemorrhagic colitis with such principal signs/symptoms as hemorrhagic diarrhea, acute abdominal cramping, vomiting, and up to hemolytic uremic syndrome (HUS).

One may ask why we have selected these abovementioned specific foodborne pathogens. We selected these because they have been enlisted as important foodborne pathogens of animal origin. Besides, food contamination brings about enormous socio-economic strain on societies. Year-in year-out, world population and across continents are affected by foodborne pathogens. Not only are chances of contamination and spread of foodborne pathogens on the rise, these pathogens enter the food chain anytime between farm and fork. With the abovementioned information in mind, subsequent sections will deal with kitchen components and its associated microbial hygiene/safety, food hygiene/microbiological safety in the typical kitchen, and human activities and participation in food hygiene/microbiological safety.Kitchen Components and Its Associated Microbial Hygiene/Safety.A well-furnished domestic kitchen will have components such as refrigerator/freezer, kitchen utensils, cabinet/cupboard, sink/basin top, table/work top, cooker, oven as well as dishwasher. The usage of these kitchen components would vary from home to home, largely dependent on such factors as family size, level of automation, income level, consciousness and effort to achieve optimum hygiene, as well as the knowledge and understanding of kitchen hygiene. A hypothetical scenario of susceptibility of microbial contamination, frequency of usage and daily cleaning routine of abovementioned kitchen components, is presented in Table 1. The ratings provided in this table are hypothetical, presenting an ideal scenario wherein any given kitchen owner would possess a optimal knowledge and understanding of (food) hygiene and microbiological safety, and wherein the individual presumes high susceptibility of microbial contamination, all put together would then be resulting in an increase in the frequency of daily cleaning routine.

Hypothetical scenario of susceptibility to microbial contamination, frequency of usage and daily cleaning routine of various kitchen components

Essentially, cross-contamination of foodborne pathogens in household kitchen are among the key contributors to global foodborne illnesses. Besides, cross-contamination by bacteria can take place in many sites in the kitchen. In line with this, cooking utensils such as knife, food processing surfaces as well as equipment/facilities used to clean the surfaces such as dishcloth, all engaged in the process of food preparation may get contaminated by any pathogen that may be present29. Also, materials that retain fewer microorganisms after cleaning would be the hygienic choice and would present a minor cross-contamination risk. For example, chopping board on a work/table top can be prone to cross-contamination particularly from juices of raw meat and poultry remaining on the surface, which result in a range of microorganisms spreading onto other foods subsequently prepared on the surface. It is possible that tear/wear can potentially affect the hygiene status of surfaces30.

When used utensils are washed in the kitchen, it is recommended that afterwards (used utensils) be kept in a (thermoset) plastic collection pack already equipped with a drain tray-like base, to allow for draining-off of water to achieve initial drying. And this (specific) tray-like base receiving the drained (out) water essentially requires regular cleaning to ensure it keeps dry. It is also recommended that (fluff-free) dishcloths be used to equally ensure that these utensils, including pots etc., are very dry before packing them away in a closed utensil drawer/shelf. And because such closed utensil drawer/shelf is most likely to be of wood types, it should be checked routinely, to make sure it stays clean, dry and odour-free. That being said, there is need for regular cleaning and drying of surfaces for such kitchen components as utensils, table/ work top, cooker, oven, dishwasher, fridge and freezer. And the use of commercially available washing-up liquids can help play a useful role in sanitizing these surfaces.

Routinely and within the stipulated time periods, refrigerators should be thoroughly cleaned so as to help sustain top-notch hygiene standards and prevent the accumulation of bad odour. And depending on frequency of usage, freezers on the other hand should be thoroughly cleaned (now and then) although the cleaning frequency in this context would be much less compared with those of refrigerators. To keep components of household kitchen at top-notch hygiene conditions even before to consider the safety of food items becomes of great necessity especially when the primary focus is to control, mitigate and prevent either disease and or infection initiation/spread. To maintain top-notch hygiene for all kitchen components requires consistency, diligence, perseverance and avoidance of procrastination. For example, washing-off used plates (immediately/shortly) after use, wiping clean the microwave (immediately/shortly) after use, drying-up kitchen utensils immediately after washing prior to keeping them in their respective spaces, should be more of a habit and routine.

Food Hygiene/Microbiological Safety (FHMS) in a Typical Kitchen

The possible sources of food contamination are well known to be numerous considering the ubiquitous nature of microorganisms. Consequently, it is common for these microorganisms to gain access to food. However, gaining access to food is one thing and growing in food is another. As mentioned previously, the fundamental target of food safety practice is to prevent either the proliferation of microorganisms and/or production of their toxins in food. Principally, the factors that affect microbial growth in foods leading to spoilage have been largely classified in terms of intrinsic, extrinsic and biotic aspects. Specifically, whilst intrinsic factors (inherent in food) involve biological structures, pH, moisture, oxidation-reduction potential, antimicrobial constituents, and nutrient content, extrinsic factors (storage environment), affecting both food and associated microorganisms, involve relative humidity, atmosphere and temperature. Biotic factors, on the other hand, involve synergism, growth rate and metabiosis31. On the other hand, it is important to note that, to be aware of food-related risks would not necessarily suffice to either incite and or motivate individuals to apply good hygiene practices. Most probably, a change in how society of the day would perceive hygiene practices may well bring about (some) increases in microbiological hazards of home-prepared food(s)

Besides, both quality and safety of food products are considered to depend highly on (storage) temperature even when considering the perspective of preparation, up to consumption stages. Either above or below freezing points, cold storage appears to be the most common existing food preservation method. Besides, the misinterpretation of food storage instruction(s) would create some avenue for a given foodborne pathogen to arise and its corresponding disease/illness risks to set in32. Therefore, for microbial growth to take place, there must be at least one viable cell even if the food (item) contains nutrients that would be sufficient to support microbial growth. This makes the fundamental aim of hygiene/microbiological safety in a kitchen very crucial, which is, to control these (abovementioned) factors, with the primary objective of reducing the number as well as presence of (pathogenic) microorganisms in food, which at the end would also be reducing the incidence/spread of foodborne illnesses.

The importance and main hazards of foodborne diseases should not be underestimated. In the USA, the cases of foodborne disease are estimated to be of greatest numbers due to known pathogens such as Norovirus, Salmonella spp., Clostridium perfringens, Campylobacter spp., and Staphylococcus aureus, whereas greatest numbers of deaths were caused by Salmonella, Toxoplasma gondii,

Listeria monocytogenes, Norovirus and Campylobacter Basically, foodborne illnesses caused by microorganisms are generally classified into two types: food infection and food intoxication. For emphasis, a food-borne illness is classified as food infection if the illness results from the consumption of live microorganisms, in food, which may grow in the body of the consumer and cause symptoms. On the other hand, it becomes (an) intoxication when the illness results from consumption of toxins produced in the food by contaminant microorganisms. Regardless, these illnesses may be avoided by knowledge of some basic facts about food safety. Factors that favor microbial growth in food have already been mentioned. Therefore, microbiological safety practices are such that counter these favorable factors to make the food unfavourable for growth of microorganisms and their activities. A few common examples are described below:

- When dishes and pots are washed in the kitchen, it is recommended that these utensils be left to dry before packing away. However, it is a common mistake in many homes for, especially lower income homes with small kitchens, to simply pack away dishes and pots after washing, without drying. There is a microbiological safety issue in this practice. Most microorganisms require moisture to grow; the more moisture there is, the more organisms can grow. If only 100 bacterial cells are deposited in a pot containing a little moisture, these 100 cells will multiply to almost 5000 cells in only six hours, whereas 1000 cells of bacteria deposited on a very dry surface would probably remain 1000 cells in the same six hours. Thus, a simple kitchen mistake such as not drying pots before storage could constitute a serious microbiological hazard in the kitchen.
- It is commonplace to prepare food much earlier before it is to be consumed, but this is also a microbiological risk in the kitchen. Storage of foods at room temperature should be avoided as much as possible. Many organisms can multiply rapidly at room temperature and just as in the example described above, a few

bacterial cells deposited in food, particularly already cooked food, can rapidly multiply to great numbers in just a few hours, becoming sources of food infection or intoxication. However, storage of the food in the refrigerator can prevent the multiplication of these cells if the organisms are not psychrophilic (cold-loving). If food has been left at room temperature for a few hours, such food should be reheated before consumption.

Achieving high level microbiological safety within the kitchen context is not too difficult, but studies have showed that there is insufficient knowledge and practice of proper kitchen hygiene among home kitchen users, thus leading to an increased prevalence of food-handling mistakes in home kitchens33. Moreover, factors that favor the outbreak of foodborne diseases can include cross-contamination, poor hygiene state of food handlers, contamination of processed foods, storage of food at ambient temperature, avoiding preparation of food in advance and improper/inadequate thawing of frozen foods31. Improper domestic food handling and unhygienic practices would be considered as vital in the extant sporadic cases of foodborne illnesses. In United Kingdom, Europe, Australia, New Zealand, United States and Canada, for example, there is evidence that up to 87% of foodborne disease outbreak would originate from food prepared or consumed at home.

Nevertheless, the definition of food safety will not change from its key aim/objective and would continue to be associated with the conditions and practices that protect the quality of food, which helps to prevent the onset of contamination as well as subsequent incidence/spread of foodborne disease/illness34. A healthy kitchen is therefore very essential in assuring high levels of food safety standards. For instance, avoiding germs is achievable by the four Cs of food safety, namely: cross-contamination, cleaning, cooking and chilling. Preventing cross-contamination ranges from washing hands before and immediately after handling raw food (e.g., meat, eggs) or after going to the toilet, disinfecting all surfaces immediately after food spillage, up to keeping pets away from food preparation/eating areas35. Therefore, scenarios where the food preparation (activity) in the household kitchen could be deduced to bring about such cross contamination and this can take place at any of its components/sites. For example, such food products as beef, lamb, pork and seafood have been considered as key sources of bacterial contamination. L. monocytogenes is well known foodborne pathogen, established within the European Union, for example Portugal, to prevail in food products like milk, meat, fish, flour and fresh cheese. Not only that the bacteria are able to adhere onto these food items/stuffs, there are equally able to serve as a potential source of contamination, which may eventually lead to disease transmission29. Particularly, the persistence of microorganisms, presence and density of pathogens and potential spread of microbial contaminants from contaminated food have been documented in scientific literature. Previously reported microbial surveys of risk of infection spread in the home considered the kitchen as highest given the significant variety of bacterial contaminants, including fecal coliforms, Escherichia coli, Campylobacter and Salmonella even after the food had been prepared.

If hand hygiene applied within the kitchen context is to become effective, there is need to ensure that various areas of hand hygiene are covered considering the fact that the 'infectious dose' of (many common) foodborne pathogens are always very small. Some key aspects include detergent-based cleaning, chemical disinfectants, drying of surfaces (decontamination), and household water treatment. Thus, hand hygiene is very essential for the reason that the hand itself is among important source of cross-contamination. This situation can arise by contact and transfer of bacteria, fungi and viruses between hand and food surfaces, which would generally result in increased risk of exposure to foodborne infection. Moreover, hygiene procedures that break the chain of infection transmission are equally very crucial. Apart from hand, there are reservoir/disseminations such as cloths, sponges, and other cleaning utensils, which if used correctly can aid detachment of particles from surfaces to remove significant proportion of soil and microbes present. There is also laundry concerns, where infection/transmission risks associated with the kitchen cloths are likely to increase, for example, in the situation that a family member is with diarrhea or vomiting or skin or wound infection. Another reservoir of microorganisms in the kitchen is the sink, given the presence of moisture that provides ideal substrate to support growth of resident microbial population. Disinfection of sink therefore is recommended when there is an infected person, or person particularly vulnerable to infection. Routine cleaning and disinfection of sink is considered as appropriate means to prevent build-up of microbial biofilms at these sites.

Many studies have considered kitchen components, small example like, sponges as a vital diffuser of pathogens that can cross-contaminate food, which inevitably serves as reservoir of food pathogens such as E. coli, Staphylococcus aureus and Salmonella spp. to thrive. And if transferred onto surfaces that are in contact with food (in the kitchen), these microorganisms have the capacity to remain viable for either hours and or days after contamination. Bacteria transfer onto other foods/surfaces easily occurs via hands/hand contact surface like cutting boards, knives and bowls. Good percentage of Salmonella spp. and Campylobacter spp. can spread to cutting boards during the preparation of naturally contaminated chicken. Salmonella. can transfer to tap handles in the same way. E. coli can transfer to contaminated cutting boards to lettuce even after overnight storage of cutting board. Most often and or always, dirty hands more or less do touch tap handles before hand washing. Essentially, hygienic cleaning of hand and food contact places help to reduce risk of cross contamination. Meanwhile, hand washing during and after food preparation remains among control measures that help to reduce the occurrence of microbiological hazards especially within a given household. In addition, the activity of cleaning ranges from decontaminating (used) kitchen items at the appropriate time to remove germs, up to encouraging the use of disposable cloths/towels. Whilst cooking meat thoroughly kills microorganisms that can result in stomach upset, chilling foods to freezing temperature slows down microbial growth.

For some time now, microbial concerns about both kitchen floor and wall have been with much debate. Besides, a (very) clean floor and wall would always demonstrate as well as reflect not only the nice appearance and welcoming household kitchen but also a (perceived) top-notch hygiene/microbiological safety level. Although it would not always be plausible for consumers (visitors, as in this instance) to have access and view a household kitchen so as to determine how clean the kitchen that have produced a given food dish is. In the situation where they have access to it, upon seeing a clean floor and wall (and presumably a very neat and well organized household kitchen), they (visitors) would certainly feel (a lot more) relaxed to consume the food dish brought before them. Hence, it would be worthwhile if future studies would pursue to fully establish how food hygiene versus cleaned kitchen environment would influence consumer feelings about food dish preparation, its consumption and even storage. Nonetheless, routine disinfection of floors has still met much opposition for the reason that it would do little to reduce cross infection risk where such exist. However, hygienic cleaning using disinfectant products continue to remain advisable in specific situations of increased risk, more specifically involving the presence of either an infected person, and or those vulnerable to infection. When spills of vomit, blood etc., have affected (kitchen) floor and walls, disinfection in addition to cleaning remain advisable.

With all above said in this section of this review, the primary aim of safe food hygiene practices still remain to remove unwanted contaminants as it can poison food, which could result in negative impact on community health.. Even at low doses, microbes can still bring about infection, for the reason that pathogens can survive starting from hours for up to weeks, and can do so on several household surfaces. Risk of human infection therefore remains an essential determinant to foodborne pathogen considering the latter's ability to persist or survive in the (food) produce even in the typical domestic/household kitchen. Implementing safe hygienic practices would therefore help in eliminating the risk of either infection and/or transmission of foodborne pathogens. Unquestionably, safety measures by consumers as final step in food preparation process are crucial in preventing foodborne illnesses and consumers' safe food handling in kitchen becomes 'the final line of defense'.

Human Activities/Participation in Food Hygiene/ Microbiological

afety (FHMS)

Some FHMS concept definitions applicable to household kitchen, snapshots of some key foodborne pathogens and corresponding diseases, kitchen components and its associated microbial hygiene/safety and food hygiene microbiological safety in kitchen have so far been discussed in this review. The next to identify with is how human carries out the activities of food hygiene /microbiological safety in the kitchen, followed by how it can be sustained. Firstly, for food as raw material to become edible and fit for purpose, there must be proper handling and preparation, which should come from the working efforts of food safety competent/qualified person(s). Secondly, how competent and/or qualified the person(s) (is/are) should remain very relative, which considers the (food hygiene/safety) training experience/expertise (already) acquired either through formal and/or informal means. Thirdly, what should be considered as more important is the person(s) to efficiently adhere to and function with the correct food hygiene/microbiological safety (FHMS) concepts/principles within the kitchen environment across the food raw material, preparation and consumption/storage stages.

To better understand the potential competences of a kitchen user as mentioned earlier, a reflection of two hypothetical scenarios would be useful. We consider two (promising) individuals 'A' and 'B': Individual 'A' from about 6-7 years of age had been extensively groomed in kitchen activities that spanned for about 15 years (informal), may well possess some equivalent food hygiene/ microbiology safety knowledge with another individual 'B' who at 17 years of age with no prior kitchen experience/training whatsoever, who has now accomplished a (formal) chef/culinary diploma training of, let's say approximately 4 years, now competent to serve in a restaurant. Undoubtedly, if at these two individual scenarios, both are to function efficiently with FHMS concepts/ principles, a clean kitchen environment must be sustained, all of which directly determines the degree of high quality safety of food raw material, preparation and consumption stages. Given these (abovementioned) contexts, we hereby propose a scheme that shows the human activity/participation during food (as) raw material, preparation, and consumption stages adding food contamination that can progress onto poisoning, all within the kitchen environment, as showed in notwithstanding that food contamination can take place at any stage(s) of food raw material, preparation, and consumption process, all of which are considered within the kitchen environment, improper / unsafe handling of raw food materials, would most likely from the very onset, increase the probability of (food) contamination and in the worst case scenario, poisoning, can subsequently take place.

poisoning, all within the kitchen environment.

A scenario that do occur across various homes can be considered here, for example, where used kitchen utensils e.g., plates, spoons, forks, etc., after dinner remain overnight in sink unwashed until next (day) morning. Not only is it a very bad household kitchen (hygiene) habit/practice, such leftover food particles can create an avenue for some (of its earlier stages of) microbial decomposition processes to start, which when it advances would result in foul odour that spoils the atmosphere of kitchen environs. Such unwashed used utensils (left in sink) can promote food contamination especially if nearby, there is unfinished food dish (in a pot and on the cooker) to be consumed the very next day (morning). Considering that cooker and sink may likely be near to each other as found in many small-like household kitchens, food contamination can take place, which may well bring about food poisoning. The start of such scenario can be when a kitchen user, in the process of washing such used utensils (if done by hand and little-to-no caution applied), may allow (without any knowledge of its occurrence) little bits of decomposing food particles finding its way between sink and cooking pot surface(s). And from that, through kitchen user's poor handling of leftover food pot, can possibly make the microbial entity on the pot surface gain entry into the food, to bring about either possible contamination and/or even poisoning in a worst case scenario. Clearly, literature has also reiterated that poor hygiene and improper food handling do pose a significant risk of food contamination as well as poisoning. Importantly, persons who handle food (food handlers) are very vital in ensuring food safety as well as preventing disease/illness situations because both poor hygiene and ineffective hand washing remain among significant risk factors of food contamination that result in food poisoning.

Thus, the food hygiene practices which consumers adopt especially while cleaning, cooking, preparation, serving and storage of food are very key in determining the root cause of large number of foodborne diseases/illnesses34. Human participation pathway to utilize food hygiene/ microbiological safety (FHMS) concepts/ principles in domestic/ household kitchen is depicted. Essentially, kitchen users should get equipped with (some) knowledge base of FHMS concepts/principles in the view to achieve its effective and efficient application onto domestic/household kitchen components. Acquiring such knowledge base should therefore be considered a pre-requisite step before such FHMS concepts/principles can be constructively, effectively and successfully utilized and sustained within the domestic/household kitchen context(s) and (extended) beyond. Indeed, consumers have a key role to play in the prevention of foodborne disease incidence. Although it is generally believed that consumers do have some awareness about appropriate steps that can prevent spread of foodborne illness/disease especially from the point of preparing up to handling of food, many yet do not put that knowledge and understanding into practice34.

A summary of some do's and don'ts of food hygiene/ microbiological safety (FHMS) applicable to domestic/household kitchen is presented . Whilst this is not an exhaustive tabulation, it is clear that there is more do's compared with don'ts. If a parent had either changed dippers or used the washroom or taking out the garbage, it is important to wash hands before and after. If gloves are worn, there should be caution because it can catch fire. Generally, cleanliness of kitchen needs to be sustained and can be achieved by observing key basic routines, for example, disposing food scraps properly and removing crumbs, wiping table tops clean with soap, sweeping and wet mopping floors, cleaning all surfaces including handles and knobs, refrigerator handles, ovens, etc. Dishcloths, aprons and towels should be laundered regularly using washing machine. Besides, cutting boards (whether it is either plastic or wood) for example should be cleaned, disinfected after use and allowed to dry properly prior to (any) re-use. Also, can openers, for example, should be cleaned thoroughly immediately after (each) use. Importantly, frozen food must be thawed either in refrigerator, microwave and oven, or by placing sealed packages in cold running water. Importantly also, all kitchen users must adhere to instructions stated, for example, on grocery packs, etc., and place those food items that require either refrigeration and/or freezing as soon as possible after purchase respectively in either refrigerator or freezer43. In addition, the essence of storing food in airtight containers is to ensure limited to zero aeration, and importantly, limited to zero exposure to any form of microbial elements. Essentially, whilst all spills should get cleaned immediately to avoid slipping and other (kitchen) accidents, it will largely minimize the incidence and spread of food pathogens

Basic/fundamental do's and don'ts of food hygiene microbiological safety applicable to domestic/household kitchen

Do's

Dont's

1. Wash hands before and after handling raw food;
2. Cover any cuts with bandage and wear clean gloves;
3. Wear hair nets to help prevent loose hair from falling on food;
4. Use utensils to serve food whenever possible;
5. Use clean spoon each time to sample/taste food;
6. Inspect kitchen for signs of microbiological growth;
7. Inspect kitchen for any plumbing leaks;
8. Use effective cleaning agents/ disinfectants;
9. Make sure cleaning materials are nearby;
10. Clean food storage area regularly especially for dry food types;
11. Always use separate cutting boards for raw meat;
12. Wash, rinse, sanitize and dry cutting boards/utensils before re-using;
13. Wash lids of canned foods before opening to keep dirt from getting into the contents;
14. Store (wet) food packages on plates to prevent its drip on kitchen work top surfaces or other food;
15. Keep cooked food warmer than 60°C (140°F) or cooler than 4°C (40°F);
16. Keep refrigerator set at 4°C (40°F);
17. Keep frozen food at – 18°C (0°F) or less;
18. Remove garbage regularly and properly;
19. Keep garbage tightly covered;
20. Food should be stored in airtight
21. containers; and Use microwave approved containers

1. Do not use aprons to dry the hands;
2. Do not smoke in the kitchen;
3. Do not store garbage in the kitchen;
4. Do not reuse any container or bowl that has held raw foods;
5. Never leave food out for more than two hours, including cut fruits and vegetables;
6. Do not keep foods too long to ensure its usage prior to expiry date;
7. Do not overstock the refrigerator;

8. Never thaw food in the kitchen table counter/ top; and
9. Do not place any cooked food in same container previously used for raw food.

Home kitchens are well known to serve, not only as storage place(s), but also as multipurpose areas. Kitchen sinks serve the purpose of dishwashing, soaking clothing, washing children, and wetting mops. Whilst food safety chain has the home as the 'last line of defense', it is believed by many that food handling errors are most likely committed by men, either adults younger than 30 years or older than 64 years, and those with at least some post-secondary education. if cleaning and sanitizing are to become very effective, it must follow a four-step process. That is to say that surfaces must be cleaned, rinsed, sanitized, and allowed to air dry. And because most foodborne illnesses appear sporadic, mild, unconfirmed and unreported, researchers believe that the cases originating from food handling errors at home could be much higher although many consumers still do not consider the home a place of risk for foodborne illnesses. Certainly, poor food hygiene practices would progress the incidence of foodborne diseases, which makes the implementation of food hygiene training very essential46. Besides, it is believed that the most food hygiene training courses may well show to rely heavily on the provision of (useful) information. If food hygiene training were to be made effective, it needs to target (some) change(s) in those behaviours that would most likely result in food-borne illness.

classification of micro – organisms.

All organisms that are very small or microscopic in size, and cannot be seen with the naked eye are referred to as microorganisms. Microorganisms are visible under the microscope. Anton van Leeuwenhoek first observed microorganisms under the microscope. Microorganisms include bacteria, archaea, algae, fungi, protozoa, etc. Although viruses are not considered living organisms, sometimes they are also included in the microorganisms category.

Classification is the process by which organisms are grouped into various categories based on morphological and physiological characteristics. There have been various attempts to classify organisms based on their morphological, physiological, cellular and molecular characteristics. Modern classification is also based on evolutionary relationships i.e. phylogenetic relationships.

Microorganisms are prokaryotic, such as bacteria, archaea,etc., as well as eukaryotic, such as protozoa, algae, fungi, etc. R.H. Whittaker elucidated the Five Kingdom Classification, which was based on the following characteristics:

- Cell type (prokaryotic and eukaryotic) and presence of nuclear membrane
- Presence of cell wall and its constituents
- Body organisation
- Mode of nutrition
- Mode of reproduction
- Phylogenetic relationships

Based on the following characteristics, R. H. Whittaker divided living organisms into five kingdoms. They are as follows:

1. Monera – Unicellular prokaryotes
2. Protista – Unicellular eukaryotes
3. Fungi – Eukaryotic, heterotrophic (saprophytic/ parasitic) and with a cell wall (chitin)
4. Plantae – Eukaryotic, autotrophic (photosynthetic) and with a cell wall (cellulose)
5. Animalia – Eukaryotic, heterotrophic (holozoic/ saprophytic etc.) and without a cell wall

Let's learn more in detail about the classification of microorganisms based on the Five Kingdom Classification.

Prokaryotic microorganisms include bacteria, cyanobacteria or blue-green algae, archaea, mycoplasma, etc. Eukaryotic microorganisms include protists, protozoans, slime moulds, algae, fungi, etc.

Bacteria (Monera)

As per the Five Kingdom Classification, bacteria are classified in the kingdom Monera. It includes Eubacteria and Archaebacteria. They are all unicellular, have a prokaryotic cell which is devoid of a membrane-bound nucleus, and other organelles such as endoplasmic reticulum, mitochondria, Golgi bodies, etc.

Later, archaebacteria were placed into a different domain of the three-domain system, i.e. Bacteria, Archaea and Eukarya.

Bacteria are the most abundant microorganisms and are present almost everywhere. They are classified as Gram-positive and Gram-negative, based on the Gram's staining pattern.

Based on the shape of the cell, bacteria are classified into four main groups that are as follows:

- Coccus or cocci (spherical)
- Bacillus or bacilli (rod-shaped)
- Spirillum or spirilla (spiral)
- Vibrium or vibrio (comma-shaped)

Eubacteria

They are true bacteria. They have a rigid cell wall and may contain flagella. They are autotrophic as well as heterotrophic. Bacteria reproduce by binary fission and DNA transfer. Some bacteria produce spores under unfavourable conditions. Mycoplasma does not contain a cell wall.

- **Photosynthetic autotrophs:** This includes blue-green algae or cyanobacteria. They contain chlorophyll 'a' similar to green plants, and perform photosynthesis. Some cyanobacteria are also capable of fixing atmospheric nitrogen. E.g. Nostoc and Anabaena.
- **Chemosynthetic autotrophs:** These microorganisms utilise energy derived from the oxidation of inorganic substances such

as nitrates, ammonia, sulphur, etc. and produce ATP. These organisms play an important role in nutrient recycling. E.g. purple sulphur bacteria.

- **Heterotrophs:** They are widely distributed and play a key role in the ecosystem as decomposers. They play a significant role in our lives. They are used for the industrial production of antibiotics, organic acids, etc. They also act as nitrogen-fixers, e.g. Rhizobium in the root nodules of legumes. Some bacteria are pathogenic to plants and animals causing various diseases, e.g. cholera, tuberculosis, typhoid, botulism, tetanus, citrus canker, fire blight of apple, etc.

Archaebacteria

They can thrive in extreme environmental conditions. They have different cell wall compositions, which enable them to survive in harsh conditions. The cell membrane of archaea is ether-linked as compared to ester-linked in bacteria. They are further classified into three main groups:

- **Methanogens** – They are found in marshy areas. They are found in the gut of many ruminating animals and are utilised for the commercial production of methane (biogas).
- **Halophiles** – They are found in extreme salty areas.
- **Thermoacidophiles** – They can tolerate extreme temperatures and low pH. They are found in hot springs.

Protozoa

In the Five Kingdom classification, protozoans are classified under the kingdom Protista, which includes unicellular eukaryotes. Protozoans are heterotrophs. They live as parasites or predators.

On the basis of their mode of locomotion, they are classified into four major groups. They are:

- **Amoeboid** – They have pseudopodia, which is used for movement and capturing prey. E.g. Amoeba, Entamoeba, etc.

- **Flagellated** – These protozoans are flagellated. They are either free-living or parasites. E.g. Trypanosoma, the causative organism of sleeping sickness, Leishmania, which causes kala-azar, etc.
- **Ciliated** – They are aquatic and have thousands of cilia present on the body surface, e.g. Paramoecium. Cilia also help in bringing water laden with food inside the cavity of the gullet.
- **Sporozoans** – They are non-motile. They produce spores. E.g. Plasmodium, the causative organism of malaria, Toxoplasma, etc.

Slime Moulds

Slime moulds are also protists. They are saprophytes. They often form aggregates called plasmodium. They form spores that are extremely resistant to adverse conditions. Slime Moulds move along dead and decaying branches and leaves, and absorb organic compounds.

Fungi

Fungi are separated into a different kingdom. They are heterotrophic and have a rigid cell wall. They are parasites or saprotrophs. Fungi are microscopic, as well as quite big in size. They are cosmopolitan and grow in warm, humid places. A unicellular fungi – yeast, is used for the industrial production of bread and alcoholic beverages. Penicillium is used for the production of antibiotics. Some fungi cause diseases in plants and animals, e.g. wheat rust (Puccinia), Candida albicans causing fungal infection in humans.

Fungi are classified into four main classes based on their morphology and method of spore formation. They are:

- **Phycomycetes** – They are characterised by the presence of coenocytic mycelium. Spores are produced endogenously in the sporangium, e.g. Rhizopus, Mucor, etc.
- **Ascomycetes** – They are commonly known as sac-fungi. The mycelium is branched and septate. The asexual spores are

produced exogenously on conidiophores and sexual spores are produced endogenously within asci. E.g. Penicillium, Saccharomyces (yeast), Aspergillus, Claviceps and Neurospora, etc.

- **Basidiomycetes** – Asexual spores are not formed. The basidiospores are exogenously produced. E.g. Puccinia (rust), mushrooms, Ustilago (smut), etc.
- **Deuteromycetes** – Commonly called imperfect fungi due to absence of sexual stage in the life cycle. Most fungi are decomposers and help in nutrient recycling. E.g. Colletotrichum, Alternaria and Trichoderma.

Algae

Unicellular photosynthetic organisms like diatoms, golden algae and dinoflagellates are placed under the kingdom Protista. They are microscopic and are plankton. They are photosynthetic and chief producers in the sea.

- **Diatoms –** They have a silicious cell wall which fits like a soap box. They are photosynthetic and 'diatomaceous earth' is used for polishing, filtration of oil, etc.
- **Dinoflagellates** – They are marine, and photosynthetic and appear in different colours. They have two unequal flagella, one longitudinal and one transverse. The cell wall has stiff cellulose plates. They are known to cause red tides due to rapid multiplication, e.g. Gonyaulax (a red dinoflagellate).

Factors affecting the growth of micro – organism.

Microorganisms are similar to more complex organisms in that they need a variety of materials from their environment to function and accomplish two primary goals--supply enough energy to manage their processes and extract building blocks to repair themselves or procreate. In addition to what they take in, microorganisms also thrive in particular environments. These environments vary as much as the organisms do themselves, and even the amount and distribution of elements in any particular environment can be very important. Scientists use this information to grow microorganisms in laboratories for experimentation.

Nutrients

All microorganisms need food. The food sources can vary, but the organisms primarily extract carbon and nitrogen from substances such as proteins, fats and carbohydrates. Some microorganisms seek out and absorb such particles. Others may perform chemical reactions with surrounding elements such as carbon dioxide to gain what they need, while still others can produce their own simple sugars through photosynthesis similar to plants. Nitrogen, which is used to synthesize proteins, can be taken from the surrounding atmosphere or from other organic matter.

Temperature

In general, the higher the temperature, the more easily microorganisms can grow up to a certain point. Very high and very low temperatures both obstruct the enzyme processes microorganisms depend on to survive, but individual species of microorganisms have grown to prefer different levels of temperature. Scientists usually divide them into three different groups: psychrophiles, mesophiles and thermophiles. Psychrophiles prefer temperatures from 0 to 5 degrees Celsius; mesophiles like it in the middle, 20-45 degrees Celsius; and thermophiles like it hot, thriving in temperatures around or above 55 degrees.

pH Levels

Microorganisms also prefer a certain pH level in the substance or environment in which they grow--that is, they prefer to have particular acidic qualities in their surroundings. Most microorganisms, including most human pathogens, are neutriphils, organisms that prefer a neutral pH level. Some like high pH levels, but most often, if conditions are too acidic, then the organism's enzymes break down.

Moisture

The free flow of water is vital to microorganisms for their cells to exchange materials and for their metabolic processes. All microorganisms require some level of water, but a few can survive in low-moisture conditions by conserving all the water they find and by staying in a moisture-rich environment. As a general rule, though, the more moisture, the more microorganisms there will be found.

Elements Present

In addition to water, microorganisms usually require the presence of certain elements in the air--gases that they absorb to produce needed nutrients. Nitrogen is one necessary element, as is oxygen. There are many microorganisms that require an oxygen-rich environment to survive, but others actually flourish in low-oxygen surroundings. Between these two extremes is a wide variety that may prefer more or less oxygen and that will be able to flourish equally no matter how much oxygen is present.

One of the very first organisms to evolve on earth was probably a unicellular organism, similar to modern bacteria. Ever since then, life has evolved into a multitude of life forms over many millennia. However, we can still trace our ancestry back to this single-celled organism.

Table of Contents

Today, bacteria are considered as one of the oldest forms of life on earth. Even though most bacteria make us ill, they have a long-term, mutual relationship with humans and are very much important for our survival. But before we elaborate on its uses, let us know the structure of bacteria, its classification, and the bacteria diagram in detail.

Bacteria Definition

"Bacteria are unicellular organisms belonging to the prokaryotic group where the organisms lack a few organelles and a true nucleus".

The bacteria diagram given below represents the structure of a typical bacterial cell with its different parts. The cell wall, plasmid, cytoplasm and flagella are clearly marked in the diagram.

Bacteria Diagram representing the Structure of Bacteria

Ultrastructure of a Bacteria Cell

The structure of bacteria is known for its simple body design. Bacteria are single-celled microorganisms with the absence of the nucleus and other **cell organelles**; hence, they are classified as prokaryotic organisms.

They are also very versatile organisms, surviving in extremely inhospitable conditions. Such organisms are called extremophiles. Extremophiles are further categorized into various types based on the types of environments they inhabit:

1. Thermophiles
2. Acidophiles
3. Alkaliphiles
4. Osmophiles
5. Barophiles
6. Cryophiles

Another fascinating feature of bacteria is their protective **cell wall**, which is made up of a special protein called peptidoglycan. The components of bacterial cell wall forms an important basis upon which the bacteria can be divided. This particular protein isn't found anywhere else in nature except in the cell walls of bacteria.

But few of them are devoid of this cell wall, and others have a third protection layer called capsule. On the outer layer, one or more flagella or pili is attached, and it functions as a locomotory organ. Pili can also help certain bacteria to attach themselves to the host's cells. They do not contain any cell organelle as in animal or plant cell except for ribosomes.

Ribosomes are the sites of protein synthesis. In addition to this DNA, they have an extra circular DNA called plasmid. These plasmids make some strains of bacteria resistant to antibiotics.

Classification of Bacteria

Bacteria can be classified into various categories based on their features and characteristics. The classification of bacteria is mainly based on the following:

- Shape
- Composition of the cell wall
- Mode of respiration
- Mode of nutrition

Also check: Bergey's Classification of Bacteria

Classification of bacteria based on Shape

Type of Classification

Examples

Bacillus (Rod-shaped)

Escherichia coli (E. coli)

Spirilla or spirochete (Spiral)

Spirillum volutans

Coccus (Sphere)

Streptococcus pneumoniae

Vibrio (Comma-shaped)

Vibrio cholerae

Classification of bacteria based on the Composition of the Cell Wall

Type of Classification

Examples

Peptidoglycan cell wall

Gram-positive bacteria

Lip polysaccharide cell wall

Gram-negative bacteria

Classification of bacteria based on the Mode of Nutrition

Type of Classification

Examples

Autotrophic Bacteria

Cyanobacteria

Heterotrophic Bacteria

All disease-causing bacteria

Classification of bacteria based on the Mode of Respiration

Type of Classification

Examples

Anaerobic Bacteria

Actinomyces

Aerobic Bacteria

Mycobacterium

Bacteria follow an asexual **mode of reproduction**, called binary fission. A single bacterium divides into two daughter cells. These are identical to the parent cell as well as to each other. Replication of DNA within the parent bacterium marks the beginning of the fission. Eventually, cell elongates to form two daughter cells.

The rate and timing of reproduction depend upon the conditions like temperature and availability of nutrients. When there is a favourable condition, E.coli or Escherichia coli produces about 2 million bacteria every 7 hours.

Bacterial reproduction is strictly asexual, but it can undergo sexual reproduction in very rare cases.

Genetic recombination in bacteria has the potential to occur through conjugation, transformation, or transduction. In such cases, the bacteria may become resistant to antibiotics since there is variation in the genetic material (as opposed to asexual reproduction where the same genetic material is present in generations)

Binary fission

Useful Bacteria

Not all bacteria are harmful to humans. There are some bacteria which are beneficial in different ways. Listed below are few benefits of bacteria:

1. Convert milk into curd – Lactobacillus or lactic acid bacteria
2. Ferment food products – Streptococcus and Bacillus
3. Help in digestion and improving the body's immunity system – Actinobacteria, Bacteroidetes, Firmicutes, Proteobacteria
4. Production of antibiotics, which is used in the treatment and prevention of bacterial infections – Soil bacteria

Antibiotics

Harmful Bacteria

There are bacteria that can cause a multitude of illnesses. They are responsible for many of the **infectious diseases**like pneumonia, tuberculosis, diphtheria, syphilis, tooth decay. Their effects can be rectified by taking antibiotics and prescribed medication. However, precaution is much more effective. Most of these disease-causing bacteria can be eliminated by sterilizing or disinfecting exposed surfaces, instruments, tools and other utilities. These methods include- application of heat, disinfectants, UV radiations, pasteurization, boiling, etc.

III

Food Hygiene & General Hygiene

Food hygiene & General hygiene : Introduction – types of food contamination – food contamination in meat, poultry, game, raw vegetables & fruits, cereals, dairy products, fish – shellfishes –destroying micro – organisms in food

Food Hygiene, otherwise known as Food Safety can be defined as handling, preparing and storing food or drink in a way that best reduces the risk of consumers becoming sick from the food-borne disease. The principles of food safety aim to prevent food from becoming contaminated and causing food poisoning. With this in mind, ensuring that food is safe for human consumption is likely the most critical part of the food preparation process. This ranges from what is called farm to fork, meaning from the farms all the way to your plate. happen. This means that food hygiene is important at home as well as in the restaurant, retail store or food factory. There has become an ever-increasing awareness of food safety by the general public and news agencies are reporting on food recalls and outbreaks much more often. Reviewing the available statistics, The CDC estimates that each year 48 million people get sick from a foodborne illness, 128,000 are hospitalised, and 3,000 die from food poisoning.

Food hygiene is important for the following reasons:

1. If food or drink is not safe to eat, you cannot eat or drink. The easiest example of this is safe drinking water. We would never drink water that did not come from a reputable source. The very same principle applies to food.
2. Every day, people worldwide get sick from the food or drink they consume. Bacteria, viruses and parasites found in food can cause food poisoning.
3. There is no immediate way of telling if food is contaminated because you cannot see, taste or smell anything different from the norm.
4. Food poisoning can lead to gastroenteritis and dehydration or potentially even more serious health problems such as kidney failure and death.
5. This risk is especially significant for those in the high-risk category: Small children/ babies, pregnant moms, the elderly and immunocompromised, especially HIV infections and cancer patients.
6. Food hygiene and safety prevent germs from multiplying in foods and reaching dangerous levels.
7. Ensures daily healthy family living.
8. Keeping one healthy and preventing the additional cost of buying medication and medical check-ups. This is especially important in business. Companies worldwide lose Billions of Dollars per year due to staff downtime.
9. Hand washing accounts for 33% of all related food poisoning cases. It is therefore important to maintain good personal hygiene practice. This is something we are taught early in our childhood, yet hand washing is still a critical problem in the kitchen

Cross-contamination is a major cause of food poisoning and can transfer bacteria from one food to another (usually raw foods to ready to eat foods).

It is crucial to be aware of how it spreads so you will know how to prevent it. Good food hygiene is therefore essential for food factories to make and sell food that is safe to eat. The first step is for the management and staff to have the knowledge and understand of what food hygiene and food safety is.

At Hygiene Food Safety we promote the food safety pillars concept which covers all aspects of food hygiene and food safety.

What Are The Food Safety Pillars?

- Cleaning & Sanitising
    - The first step in creating a food safety system is the fundamental aspect of cleaning and sanitising.
- Personal Hygiene
    - The second pillar is probably the most important in terms of eliminating cross-contamination. Hand washing and clean hands awareness are critical to food safety.
- Food Storage
- The third pillar can be categorised into two areas
    - Perishable foods (Cold storage)
    - Dry goods
- Temperature Control
    - The fourth pillar of food safety is a fundamental principle in preventing the growth of bacteria and ensuring the quality of food is maintained.
- Food Handling

- The fifth and final pillar of food safety related to how food is handled during storage and preparation. Food Handling carries the greatest risk when dealing with cross-contamination.

Using the food safety pillars is an essential way to prevent food poisoning. This system can be used in any kitchen, whether at home, hotel, restaurant, food truck or food factory.

How to practice food hygiene at home

Practice Good Personal Hygiene

Personal hygiene is a practice everyone should have. It is important to always wash your hands with soap and water before handling food to prepare.

Clean Utensils and Cooking Equipment

All cooking equipment should be properly cleaned and sanitised before starting any preparation. This is specifically important for equipment that comes into direct contact with food. Such as cutting boards, knives, countertops, mixers, blenders etc. These areas are known to harbour dangerous bacteria that when they get into foods that cause serious illness. All utensils and crockery need to be cleaned for the same reasons.

Keep Foods That Need to be Kept Cold in the Fridge:

Raw meats, dairy and others need to be kept cold (4°C – 39°F) in order to prevent bacteria from growing before you can consume the food. Keeping foods cold also ensures that your food does not expire before the use-by dates.

Separate Raw and Ready to Eat Foods

By its very nature, raw foods have bacteria present in them. This is why we need to cook most of our foods. There is no way you can keep cooked foods together with the raw. Foods such as meat, fish and fruits, soup and stew should be refrigerated/frozen in different sealed containers and they should be kept in a different compartment of the fridge to avoid cross-contamination which can occur through dripping.

After marinating fish or meat, do not use the same bowl or plate to serve food or place another food into it, you can only use the sauce to cook food but not to serve as food because it is raw and it will be unhealthy for your consumption.

Wash Fruits and Vegetables Before Use

Most fruits and vegetable are freshly purchased from the farm, store or market; these foods contain soil, insects and chemical residues in them, it is very important to rinse vegetables and fruit with water, salt or vinegar before storing them in the food rack.

Use Appropriate Kitchen Tools for Food Preparation

There are various kinds of kitchen tools/utensils designed for different purposes, make sure you use the right tool at the right time. For instance, a meat chopping board can easily serve as a growth medium for bacteria and mould, this can be seen growing on the surface or the edges if not properly washed after usage, use a different chopping board for cutting vegetables and other sensitive foods to prevent food poisoning and always wash and disinfect cutting tools.

Keep Dry Foods Separate From Liquids

Food safety should include dry goods such as grains, dried and powdered foods storage. Wet food attracts moulds easily. Grains, powdered, baked, and canned or dry foods should be properly stored away from liquid, as moulds can easily grow on them causing illness, allergy and food poisoning to both adults and kids.

Cook Food to an Appropriate Temperature

Cooking food to the required temperature is an important food safety practice, as raw foods like egg and meat can easily result in Salmonella and E.coli infections if not properly cooked. Foods such as pork, chicken, beef and processed meats like sausage should be cooked longer until there are no traces of pink on the flesh and joints and bones of such meats because bacteria can easily survive the cooking process in these areas.

Keep Insects and Pests Away From Food Areas

Insects and pests control is another important food hygiene tip to be taken into consideration, as these creatures are often seen in our houses, especially in places like the fridge corners, kitchen cupboard, shelves and at dark corners of the kitchen. Cockroaches, flies and rodents as we know are very terrible insects and pest; they can carry pathogens from one surface to another, which can lead to food-borne illness, for this reason, it is wise to always cover the pots containing foods, spray the shelves, clean our refrigerator when you notice any foul smell and dripping.

Always Use Clean Water to Prepare Food

Food hygiene is also an important practice to be carried out when washing, mixing and cooking food. Water has many ways of affecting our systems and our general health. Foods that are prepared with unsafe water can easily lead to vomiting, diarrhoea and stomach upsets, it is important to always use clean water to wash and cook food.

Clean the Kitchen and Mop the Floor After Each Food Preparation:

Keeping the kitchen clean can help keep flies, ants and cockroaches from coming in contact with your foods. Greasy areas help bacteria hide and cannot be eliminated without removing the grease. The stove or gas top should be properly wiped.

Keep Kitchen Towels, Sponges and Cleaning Cloths Clean and Replace Regularly

The kitchen and every tool or equipment in it should be washed and sanitised. Kitchen towels or sponges are very important items in the kitchen and are used on a daily basis to open hot lids, remove foods from the microwave or oven, bring down boiling soup from heat and wipe off food or water from our wet hands. Often times while using these towels, they get wet in the process which means that microorganisms can harbour on these damp surfaces, so it will be very proper to wash and sanitise and properly.

At are good personal hygiene habits?

Good personal hygiene includes but not limited to-

- Take regular shower
- Maintain oral hygiene

- Wash your hands frequently
- Wash your genitals
- Keep your clothes and surrounding dry and clean

These habits should be practiced on a regular basis, at home, at work, basically where you are! That's the whole idea of preventing your body system collapse over a tiny microbe!

Personal Hygiene Practices at Home

Your home should be the most comfortable and convenient for you to keep up your personal hygiene level to a standard, yet, we find ourselves procrastinating over hygiene issues when we are at home. Even though some of these tasks barely take a minute.

1. Take Regular shower

Do not wait up to feel the dried sweat in your body to feel the urge to take shower, make it a routine, you have the choice to either take them before you head to work or after the long day or even before you head to sleep, whichever one suits your routine. Make sure to rinse your body thoroughly, especially the genitals and underarms as they produce more sweat and are more prone to fungal activities.

2. Wash your hands frequently

It is our hands that we use to do our most physical acts, from picking up the keys, browsing through our phones to attending our pets. While we acknowledge the importance of washing hands before eating and after visiting the toilet, it is also **important to wash our hands** with soap or sanitizer every now and then.

3.Maintain oral hygiene practices

Caring for your teeth and gum is important, not only to prevent decay related issues but also as they affect neurologically some other sensual organs, they shouldn't be taken in a light manner. Just brushing them twice a day is not enough, make sure you are using fluoride toothpaste and brushing properly.

Also, you should floss after eating, as this practice will remove plaque, bacterial, and debris that was trapped between teeth which your toothbrush cannot reach. It is a great way to prevent bad breath too. Don't hesitate to pay a visit to your dentist in slightest discomfort.

. Trim your nails and wash your hairs

Your nails and hair store dirt and grease. None not to mention the microbes could be in there stuck and spreading. Bad nail hygiene can cause severe food poisoning since you would be preparing or eating your food with your hands. Trim the nails every once they are inappropriately long and wash your hairs at least twice a week to keep them healthy.

5. Clean your nose and ears

Every time you are outside, you are most likely to breathe in some pollutants, and most of the particles are bound to be stuck in your nasal hair. You should rinse your nose and ear with warm water upon return. Especially if you have any specific allergies.

6. Wear fresh and warm clothes

Try to change into some warm and dry clothes, you'll feel the mental effect immediately as they will boost your mind. Also, regular washing with right detergent matters since like your body, your clothes can be contaminated with germs or microbes, especially if they have been used for several days.

7. Food hygiene is important too

You can get severely sick from food-borne diseases, as most of your foods are raw, purchased from outside, they risk being cross-contaminated with harmful microbes.

Read More: Why Food Hygiene is Important?

Food hygiene is basically the idea of better storage, handling, and preparation of food to prevent contamination causing food poisoning. **Here are a few points to note while handling food:**

- Use separate storage units for liquid and solid foods at appropriate temperature.
- Wash vegetables and fruits with clean water before consuming and storing.
- Keep utensils and cooking tools clean and sanitised.
- Prepare raw food at an appropriate temperature.

- Always wash your hands with soap and water before handling food.
- Maintain a clean kitchen and keep foods away from pests and insects.

Personal Hygiene Practices for Kids

et's face it, kids are kids, and you can't expect them to preside over some "hygiene" issues and it's a never ending battle. Yet, they are more vulnerable to suffer due to bad hygiene practice.

These above-discussed practices are not only for adults to incorporate in their life. So, it is your duty to make them understand the importance of good personal hygiene. At the same time, try to instill better self-awareness in them. You can practice hygiene habits yourself, like brushing twice a day, bathing regularly, and washing hands after using the toilet and before eating and they follow.

By laying out ground rules early and making sure your kids follow them, you'll start seeing them take care of their hygiene issues.

Maintaining Workplace Hygiene

Like your home and body, your workplace can provide access for parasites and germs to get to you. But here you come into contact with many people every day, and there is always a bigger risk of being contaminated through them.

- Installing and carrying hand sanitizer is highly recommended.
- Use recycle bins appropriately, if not available, initiate talk to get them installed.
- Use the designated area for lunch and clean afterwards.
- Raise awareness among your colleagues of the benefits of good personal hygiene.
- Keeping your surroundings neat and clean can be a deal-breaker as it will promote a better working environment both for your mind and body.

- Allow and encourage sick days even if it's apparently just a cold. It's better to have one employee get some rest than spreading the flu in the whole workplace.

You can't change yourself into a hygiene freak in one day and we're not asking you to be. It's about taking these conscious steps to make your personal hygiene better or help your kid develop better habits. You can start by setting reminders, signs or cues to do a certain activity, do it for a week or two and you will get accustomed to it.

Our Most Common Types of Food Contamination

By KENT RO SYSTEMSVeg & Fruit Purifier4 Comments

ruits and vegetables are an integral part of our diet. However, over the years, the use of **pesticides** and **insecticides** has increased drastically, which also raises the risk of a number of health problems. Apart from pesticides, there are a number of other scenarios that may lead to **food contamination**. Though we are extra cautious when it comes to handling food items, rinsing them with plain water doesn't serve the purpose. Many of us are not aware that **food contamination** is divided into four categories, all of which may lead to serious health problems. As a result, it is necessary to ditch the age-old procedures of **washing fruits and vegetables** and bring home a vegetable and fruit cleaner. The advanced appliance uses **ozone disinfection technology** to help you remove pesticides and contaminants from food items. If you are not aware of the different types of contaminants, we are here to help. The blog describes in detail the four different types of **food contamination** that you need to know.

What is Food Contamination?

Food contamination is a commonly used term. However, only a few people are aware of the exact reasons for food contamination and its effects on your health. When food items are not handled or cooked safely, the disease-causing organisms such as bacteria, parasites, and viruses result in food contamination. The disease-causing parasites produce toxins that may also lead to food intoxication. In addition, the presence of pesticides, and certain cleaning compounds, contaminate the food. The common reasons for food contamination are:

- Improper storing, handling, and preparing food
- Improperly cleaned or sanitized utensils
- Contamination by flies, cockroaches, insects, and pests

Major Four Types of Food Contamination

There are a number of reasons that can lead to **food contamination**. However, food contamination falls under four different categories which are:

- Biological contamination
- Chemical contamination
- Physical contamination
- Cross-contamination

Read on to find out more about the different **types of food contamination** and their effect on your health.

1. Biological Contamination

Biological contamination is one of the common causes of food poisoning as well as spoilage. **Contamination of food items by other living organisms is known as** biological food contamination. During biological contamination, the harmful bacteria spread on foods that you consume. Even a single bacterium can multiply very quickly when they find ideal growth conditions. Not just **bacteria**, but also their process of multiplying can be quite harmful to humans. The common places where you can find bacteria are:

- Dust
- Raw meat
- The air
- The human body
- Pets and pests

- Kitchen clothes

The best way to avoid food contamination is by washing the food items with **KENT vegetable and fruit cleaner** and washing the kitchen cloths regularly.

2. Physical Contamination

When harmful objects contaminate the food it leads to **physical contamination.** At times, food items can have both physical and **biological contamination**. Some of the safety tips that you can follow when handling food items to prevent food contamination are:

- Hair-Tie your hair when handling food
- Glass or Metal-Clean away cracked or broken crockery and utensils to avoid contamination
- Dirt-**KENT Vegetable and Fruit Cleaner** helps in removing dirt from fruits and vegetables
- Jewellery-Wear minimum jewellery when preparing food

3. Chemical Contamination

Chemical contaminants are one of the serious sources of food contamination. These contaminants can also lead to food poisoning. Pesticides present in fruits and vegetables are one of the main sources of contamination. In addition, kitchen cleaning agents, food containers made of non-safe plastic, pest control products also lead to food contamination. Though we make it a point to wash fruits and vegetables thoroughly, however, plain water can't remove all the contaminants. This is where KENT Vegetable and Fruit Disinfectant can help you out. The smart kitchen appliance uses **ozone disinfection technology** that helps you removes contaminants from the surface of the fruits and vegetables to make it safe for consumption.

4. Cross-Contamination

Many of us are not aware of cross-contamination; however, this type of contamination can lead to a number of health problems.

Cross-contamination takes place when pathogens are transported from any object that you use in the kitchen. Dirty kitchen clothes, unclean utensils, pests, raw food storage can lead to cross-contamination. Here are some of the ways to avoid cross-contamination:

- **Utensils**- Use separate utensils to prepare different types of foods. Avoid using the same chopping board and knife for ready to eat foods
- **Storing Food**- Make sure raw foods don't come in contact with ready to eat foods. Cover and store raw foods below cooked foods to prevent cross-contamination.
- **Disposing Waste**- Make sure you store and seal garbage correctly to prevent cross-contamination. Clean and sanitize the waste bins to prevent infestation risk.

Who is at a Higher Risk of Food Poisoning?

Though anyone can get food poisoning, some age groups are at a higher risk. The following age groups are at a higher risk of food poisoning.

1. Kids who are Younger than 5 Years

Kids who are less than 5 years have a weak immune system and their body's ability to fight infections is less. Food poisoning can be very dangerous for children as it leads to dehydration and diarrhea. Children, less than 5 years are three times more likely to be hospitalized by food poisoning.

2. Pregnant Women

Expectant mothers are more vulnerable to certain germs as compared to others. This is the reason why pregnant women are 10 times more vulnerable to food poisoning than other people.

3. Elderly People

Adults who are more than 65 years of age are at a higher risk of food contamination as their immune systems are weak. Their organs don't recognize and get rid of harmful germs present in food items, making them vulnerable to food poisoning.

4. People with Weak Immune System

A weak immune system makes harder for your body to fight disease and as a result they are more likely to get food poisoning and have serious health effects. People suffering from diseases such as diabetes, high blood pressure, kidney or liver disease have a low immunity level and they are not in the condition to fight germs and sicknesses. This is the reason why they are at a higher risk of suffering from food poisoning. These people are at a higher risk of suffering from serious complications, including death.

How to Reduce the Risk of Food Poisoning?

To lower the chance of getting affected by food poisoning it is very important that you must be careful about what you are eating, how you are storing, washing and preparing your food. The most important thing that one should follow is to wash fruits, vegetables, raw meat, poultry, fish and seafood properly before consumption. Simple washing with tap water may not be effective enough to remove the harmful germs and chemicals from the surface of the eatables and consuming it can cause severe food poison.

This is where the use of KENT Vegetable and Fruit Cleaner comes to play. Though we are very careful when handling food, however, there are many other ways through which food may get contaminated, which may go unnoticed. As a result, it is always a good idea to use a vegetable and fruit cleaner from KENT to wash the food items before cooking to ensure that you are eating safely. The smart appliance uses powerful ozone technology to sterilize the fruits and vegetables and make it fit for consumption. This revolutionary technology can kill bacteria, viruses, fungi and other pathogens that are present on the surface of the food items that may lead to food borne diseases. More importantly, it can even help you remove insecticides, pesticides and chemicals from vegetables, fruits and meat and ensure that whatever you cook is safe for consumption.

Some foods are more associated with foodborne illnesses and food poisoning than others. They can carry harmful germs that can make you very sick if the food is contaminated.

- Raw foods of animal origin are the most likely to be contaminated, specifically raw or undercooked meat and poultry, raw or lightly cooked eggs, unpasteurized (raw) milk, and raw shellfish.
- Fruits and vegetables also may get contaminated.
- While certain foods are more likely to make you sick, any food can get contaminated in the field, during processing, or during other stages in the food production chain, including through cross-contamination with raw meat in kitchens.

Learn more about the foods that are more associated with food poisoning and how to avoid getting sick from them:

Chicken, Beef, Pork, and Turkey

Thoroughly cooking chicken, poultry products, and meat destroys germs.

Raw and undercooked meat and poultry can make you sick. Most raw poultry contains Campylobacter. It also may contain Salmonella, Clostridium perfringens, and other bacteria. Raw meat may contain Salmonella, E. coli, Yersinia, and other bacteria.

- You should not wash raw poultry or meat before cooking it, even though some older recipes may call for this step. Washing raw poultry or meat can spread bacteria to other foods, utensils, and surfaces, and does not prevent illness.
- Thoroughly cook poultry and meat. You can kill bacteria by cooking poultry and meat to a safe internal temperature.
- Use a cooking thermometer to check the temperature. You can't tell if meat is properly cooked by looking at its colour or juices.
- Leftovers should be refrigerated at 40°F or colder within 2 hours after preparation. Large cuts of meat, such as roasts or a whole turkey, should be divided into small quantities for refrigeration so they'll cool quickly enough to prevent bacteria from growing.

Foodborne Germs and Poultry and Meat

- E. coli and Food Safety
- Salmonella and Food
- Prevent Illness from Clostridium Perfringens

Tips for Preparing Chicken, Turkey, and Other Meats

- Preparing Your Holiday Turkey Safely
- How to Grill Safely
- Safe Minimum Cooking Temperatures Chart
- The Raw Story: Frozen Chicken Entrees

The safest fruits and vegetables are cooked; the next safest are washed. Avoid unwashed fresh produce.

Eating fresh produce provides important health benefits, but sometimes raw fruits and vegetables may cause food poisoning from harmful germs such as Salmonella, E. coli, and Listeria. Fresh fruits and vegetables can be contaminated anywhere along the journey from farm to table, including by cross-contamination in the kitchen

Tips for Fruits and Vegetables

- Fruit and Vegetable Safety
- Fresh Fruits, Vegetables, and Juices
- external icon
- Lettuce, Other Leafy Greens, and Food Safety

Raw Milk, Raw Milk Soft Cheeses, and Other Raw Milk Products

To prevent infection with Listeria and other harmful germs, don't consume raw milk or soft cheeses and other products made from raw milk.

You can get very sick from raw (unpasteurized) milk and products made with it, including soft cheeses (such as queso fresco, blue-veined, feta, brie and camembert), ice cream, and yogurt. That's because raw milk can carry harmful germs, including Campylobacter, Cryptosporidium, E. coli, Listeria, and Salmonella.

- Raw milk is made safe through pasteurization, which requires just enough heat for just long enough to kill disease-causing germs.
- Most of the nutritional benefits of drinking raw milk are also available from pasteurized milk, without the risk.
- Although Listeria infection is very uncommon, it can sicken pregnant women, older adults, and people with weakened immune systems.
- Listeria infection can cause miscarriages, stillbirths, preterm labour, and serious illness and even death in newborns.

Learn About the Dangers of Raw Milk and Soft Cheeses

- Raw (Unpasteurized) Milk
- Raw Milk Know the Facts
- Milk, Cheese, and Dairy Products
- Listeriosis Outbreaks Linked to Soft Cheeses

Eggs and Salmonella

Cook eggs until the yolks and whites are firm.

Eggs can contain a germ called Salmonella that can make you sick, even if the egg looks clean and uncracked. Use pasteurized eggs and egg products when preparing recipes that call for raw or undercooked eggs. In addition:

- Avoid foods that contain raw or undercooked eggs, such as homemade Caesar salad dressing and eggnog.
- Cook eggs until the yolks and whites are firm.
- Cook foods containing eggs thoroughly.
- Keep eggs refrigerated at 40°F or colder.
- Do not taste or eat raw batter or dough.

Tips for Preparing and Eating Eggs

- Salmonella and Eggs

- Eggs and Egg Products

Seafood and Raw Shellfish

Raw or undercooked oysters can contain Vibrio bacteria, which can lead to an infection called vibriosis.

Cook seafood to 145°F, and heat leftover seafood to 165°F. To avoid foodborne infection, do not eat raw or undercooked fish, shellfish, or food containing raw or undercooked seafood, such as sashimi, some sushi, and ceviche.

Oysters and Food Poisoning

- Oysters and other filter-feeding shellfish can contain viruses and bacteria that can cause illness or death.
- Oysters harvested from contaminated waters can contain norovirus.
- To avoid food poisoning, cook oysters well.

Food Safety for Seafood and Oysters

- Oysters and Vibriosis
- Seafood

Sprouts

Cook sprouts thoroughly to reduce the chance of food poisoning.

The warm, humid conditions needed to grow sprouts are also ideal for germs to grow. Eating raw or lightly cooked sprouts, such as alfalfa, bean, or any other sprout, may lead to food poisoning from Salmonella, E. coli, or Listeria. Thoroughly cooking sprouts kills the harmful germs and reduces the chance of food poisoning.

Raw Flour

You should never taste raw dough or batter.

Flour is typically a raw agricultural product that hasn't been treated to kill germs. Harmful germs can contaminate grain while it's still in the field or at other steps as flour is produced. Bacteria are killed when food made with flour is cooked. That's why you should never taste raw dough or batter.

- Say No to Raw Dough
- Flour, Raw Dough, and Raw Batter
- Fruit and Vegetable

Eating a diet with plenty of fruits and vegetables gives many health benefits. But it's important to select and prepare them safely.

Fruits and vegetables add nutrients to your diet that help protect you from heart disease, stroke, and some cancers. Also, choosing vegetables, fruits, and nuts over high-calorie foods can help you manage your weight.

Sometimes, raw fruits and vegetables contain harmful germs that can make you and your family sick, such as Salmonella, E. coli, and Listeria. CDC estimates that germs on fresh produce cause a large percentage of foodborne illnesses in the United States.

The safest produce to eat is cooked; the next safest is washed. You can enjoy uncooked fruits and vegetables by taking the following steps to reduce your risk of foodborne illness, also known as food poisoning.

Contamination source of cereal products

- Air and dust
- Soil
- Water
- Insects
- Rodents
- Birds
- Animals
- Humans
- environmental conditions (such as drought, rainfall, temperature, and sunlight)
- harvesting and processing equipment
- Contaminated equipment and unsanitary handling.
- Storage condition and storage temperature

- Shipping containers

Spoilage of cereal

- Cereals usually contain 70–75% carbohydrates, 8–15% protein, fat, fiber, vitamins, and minerals with near-neutral pH and hence are susceptible to microbial growth leading to spoilage.
- Microbial growth is normally prevented due to sufficiently low water activity (i.e. below 0.70).
- Mold is considered the primary organism for causing spoilage in cereal.
- Bacteria can also cause spoilage of cereals, but yeasts cause few spoilage problems.
- The most commonly associated bacterial families with cereals are Bacillaceae, Micrococcaceae, Lactobacillaceae, and Pseudomonadaceae.
- Yeast that is found in cereal includes Candida, Cryptococcus, Pichia, Sporobolomyces, Rhodotorula, Trichosporon
- Mold spores in cereals and flour are chiefly Aspergillus, Penicillium, Alternaria, Mucor, Cladosporium, Fusarium, Helminthosporium, Cladosporium, and Rhizopus.
- Mycotoxins are the toxic secondary metabolites produced by mold that is found in cereal crops under favorable growth conditions. The genera of molds producing mycotoxins are Aspergillus, Penicillium, and Fusarium.
- A high incidence of mycotoxin infections in cereals has been observed worldwide.

Some examples of mycotoxin and the mold that produce them are:

S.No

Mold

Mycotoxin

1

Aspergillus parasiticus

Aflatoxins B1, B2, G1, G2,

2

Aspergillus flavus

Aflatoxins B1, B2

Penicillium islandicum

Islanditoxin, luteoskyrin

Fusarium sporotrichioides

Trichothecenes: T-2 toxin

Some of the microorganisms and the defects caused by them in cereals are

Microorganisms

Defects in cereal

Alternaria, Fusarium, Drechslera, Cladosporium, and Botrytis

Blights and blemishes

Aspergillus fumigatus, A. penicillioides, A. ochraceus

Discolored germs

A. candidus

Powdery white patches

A. flavus

Greenish discoloration

Eurotium

Discolored germs, green eye

Fusarium

Red streaking, particularly on maize

Penicillium

Blue coloration

Alternaria

Darkening

Fusarium or Alternaria

Pink or black tips in wheat

Claviceps purpira

Ear rot (ergotism) in grain and corn

Preservation of cereal

Pesticides

- The chemicals used to prevent and control the occurrence of pests causing harm to crops that includes including fungicides, herbicides, and insecticides.
- The pesticides provide crop protection from the damaging influences of pests, higher yields, and better quality of cereals.

Drying

- Grains are dried to a low moisture content until the moisture content level guaranteeing safe storage conditions(i.e. equivalent to <0.70 aw)
- Drying helps to create unfavorable conditions for mold growth and the proliferation of insects.

Debranning

- Debranning is a process during which the bran layers are removed.
- This technique is found to improve the yield and degree of refinement of flour, as well as allowing the production of good quality grains.
- After debranning, grains are found to be microbiologically purer as the total microbial contamination was reduced up to 87%.

Chlorine and hypochlorite

- The chlorine-based methods are widely used in cereal for microbial control.
- Sodium hypochlorite has also been used frequently.

Irradiation

- It is a process that involves exposing cereal food to a certain amount of ionizing radiation.

- Irradiation has been successfully used for the control of microorganisms on cereals and flours.

Ozone

- Ozone (O3) is the triatomic oxygen formed by the addition of a free radical of oxygen to molecular oxygen.
- The use of ozone as a fungicide for decontamination of cereal grains has been investigated in several studies.

Microwave (MW) treatment

- Microwaves are electromagnetic waves with frequencies within 300 MHz to 300 GHz.
- It is widely used for the inactivation of microorganisms associated with cereal grains.
- Microwave energy can also be used for the control of stored grain insects.

Pulsed ultraviolet (UV) light treatment

- Pulsed UV light treatment is a non-thermal technology that can be used both for decontamination of foods and food contact surfaces.
- Pulsed UV light is considered to be more efficient in microbial inactivation than UV light, offering safer and faster decontamination.
- The antimicrobial efficacy of this technology against microorganisms occurring on stored cereal grains has been studied.

Non-thermal (cold) plasma

- Cold plasma can be generated at atmospheric as well as low pressure and consists of UV photons, neutral or excited atoms and molecules, negative and positive ions, free radicals, and free electrons.

- As a non-thermal process, cold plasma does not cause damage to the food product after treatment.
- This process has shown the inactivation of two pathogenic fungi, Aspergillus spp. and Penicillium spp. in cereals.
- This process has also shown the inactivation of Geobacillus stearothermophilus and Bacillus amyloliquefaciens.

Organic acid

- Organic acids are used as food additives and preservatives and can also be used for grain preservation.
- Adding organic acids (acetic, citric, lactic, or propionic) or a combination of organic acids and NaCl added to tempering water is found to reduce microbial contamination in cereal.
- It was reported that the combination of lactic acid (5.0%) and NaCl (52%) was the most effective against aerobic plate count and Enterobacteriaceae.

Spoilage of cereal products
Flour spoilage

- The moisture content of the flour is less than 13% that prevents the growth of microorganisms.
- However, the addition of water to flour tends to make it susceptible to microbial growth in flour.
- The molds found in flours are mostly Eurotium species and Aspergillus candidus. The molds produce typical mycelium in flour.
- The spoilage flour contains many psychrotrophs, flat sour bacteria, and thermophilic spore-forming bacteria such as Acetobacter spp, Bacillus spp, Lactic acid bacteria.
- If acid-forming bacteria are present in flour, acid fermentation occurs followed by alcoholic fermentation by yeasts and then

acetic acid by Acetobacter spp.

- Bacillus spp is known for producing lactic acid, gas, and acetoin in flour.

Preservation of flour

- Flour can be preserved in an air-tight container for 6-10 months and a vacuum-packed container for 1-2 years.
- It can also be preserved in the freezer.
- It can also be preserved by filling it in oxygen absorbers containers for a long shelf-life of flour.

SOURCES OF CONTAMINATION IN MILK

Introduction

Milk when secreted into an uninfected animals udder is sterile and invariably, it becomes contaminated during milking, cooling and/or storage. It is an excellent medium for the growth of bacteria, yeasts and moulds that are the common contaminants of any food material. Their rapid growth, particularly at high ambient temperatures can spoil the milk for liquid consumption and for manufacturing dairy products. This can be avoided to a greater extent by adopting the basic rules of clean milk production.

Sources of Microbial Contamination of Milk

Microbial contamination of milk can be from the internal and/ or external sourcesthat are described in the following section.

Interior of udder

Varying numbers of bacteria are found in aseptically drawn milk with the reported counts of <100-10,000 CFU/ml from normal udder, but an anticipated average is 500-1000 CFU/ml in advanced countries. Microorganisms enter the udder through the duct at the teat tip that varies in length (from 5-14 mm) and its surface is heavily keratinized. This keratin layer retains the milk residues and exhibit antimicrobial activity.

During progress of a milking, bacteria are present in the largest numbers at the beginning and then gradually decrease. This is mainly due to the mechanical dislodging of bacteria, particularly in teat canal, where the numbers are probably highest. Because of this discarding of first few streams of milk helps in lowering the counts of microbes in milk. Milk from different quarters also vary in numbers.Different species of bacteria that are found in milk, as it comes from udder are very limited as given in

Presence of different microbial groups in raw milk

Though micrococci are slow growing, but if allowed to grow, they cause acid formation and proteolysis. These are mostly non-pathogenic. Streptococci are less frequent than micrococci. Streptococcus agalactiae may be present even in non-clinical mastitis and thus it appears to be a natural inhabitant of udder. Among Gram positive rods, Corynebacterium bovis has been found in large numbers. It is non-pathogenic, but if grown causes rancidity. If an animal is infected from mastitis, microbial contamination from within the udder of animal contributes notably to the total numbers of microbes in the bulk milk, when compared with the milk originated from a healthy animal. The influence of mastitis on the total bacterial count of milk depends on the type of the infecting microbe. Most common microbial agents of mastitis in milch animals are given in are Staphylococcus aureus, Streptococcus agalactiae, Streptococcus dysgalactiae, Streptococcus uberis, Escherichia coli and Corynebacterium pyogenes.

Most common microbial agents of mastitis

Exterior of udder

In addition, to the udder infections, unclean udder and teats of animal also contribute significantly to the total bacterial counts of milk. The microbes that are naturally associated with the skin of the animals as well as those derived from the environment, where the cow is housed and milked are predominant in the milk. The environmental conditions such as soil, manure, mud, feed or bedding; determines what kind of microbes will dominate in milk.

1. Udder and teat become soiled with dung, mud, bedding material such as saw dust, straw etc. With heavily soiled udder teats the

counts may be 1,00,000 cfu/ml. The bedding material in winter has high number of bacteria, mainly psychrotrophs, coliforms and Bacillus spp. Udder microflora is not affected much by simple washing. Economy washing with sodium hypochlorite accompanied by drying, helps in reducing the number of microbes. Different category of microbes that occurs in the exterior of udder are

- Predominantly micrococci and coagulase negative staphylococci exist.
- Next, on the teat surface are faecal streptococci, but Gram negative bacteria including coliforms are less. Coliforms do not survive well on teat surface.
- Aerobic thermoduric organisms are entirely Bacillus spp. The more frequent are B. licheniformis, B. subtilis, B. pumilis and less frequent ones are B. cereus, B. circulans and B. firmus.
- Teat surface may also contain clostridial spores that are usually found in cows fodder, bedding and faeces.

Psychrotrophic and thermoduric bacteria predominate on the teat surfaces. The psychrotrophs that can grow at 7C and below are mostly Gram negative rods, and the major ones are Pseudomonas fluorescens, followed by Alcaligenes, Flavobacterium and coliforms On the other hand, thermodurics on teat surfaces are often bacterial spores (a dormant and non-reproductive structure; highly resistant to radiations, desiccation, lysozymes, high temperature, starvation and disinfectants) that are typically found in the soil.When these spores enter the bulk milk, they may survive during pasteurization and cause a number of post-pasteurization problems.

Coat of cow

Thecoat serves as a vehicle to contribute bacteria directly to milk. The hairs around udder, flanks and tail contribute to the higher bacterial count in milk. The coat may indirectly contribute microbes into air, especially Bacillus spp. The coat may carry bacteria from the stagnant water pools, especially ropiness causing milk microbes.

Animal shed and surroundings

Milk produced on farms with poor hygiene practices may undergo significant spoilage and have a shorter shelf-life, when compared to milk produced under hygienic conditions. Microbes associated with the bedding materials include:

1. Coliforms
2. Spore-formers
3. Staphylococci
4. Streptococci
5. Other Gram negative bacteria

Milking staff

The staffs involved at different stages of milk production plays a pivotal role in maintaining hygiene and preventing milk contamination. The hand contacts or dislodging of dust and dirt particles by milker may add varieties of microbes to milk. Risks of contamination from milker are definitely higher, when cows are hand-milked in comparison to when they are machine-milked. Soiled clothes and hands increase the risk of contamination of milk and milking equipments many folds. Milker with infected wounds on hands contributes pathogenic Streptococcus spp. and micrococci. If wet hand milking is practiced, the microorganisms present in lubricants like fore-milk, water or saliva of the milker and bacteria from hands and teats will enter the milk.

The common microbial pathogens from humans causing diseases such as typhoid, paratyphoid and dysentery may contaminate the milk. Microbial pathogens causing scarlet fever, septic sore throat, diptheria, cholera etc. contaminate the milk.

Milking equipment (storage containers and transportation systems)

Improperly cleaned milking and cooling equipments are one of the main sources of milk contamination. Milk residues left on the equipment contact surfaces supports the growth of a variety of microbes. Although natural inhabitants of the teat canal, apex and skin; microorganisms associated with contagious mastitis do not grow well on these equipments, it is possible that certain strains associated with environmental mastitis may grow to a significant level. Since, it is very difficult to remove all milk residues and deposits from the milk contact surfaces of milking equipments; hence equipment with smooth surfaces and minimal joints should be used. The tanker and collecting pipes are also the potential sources of contamination, if not adequately cleaned. In addition, biofilms can easily build up on the enclosed, hard to clean surfaces .

Unclean or improperly cleaned milk cans and lids if they are still moist, results in multiplication of thermophilic bacteria like Bacillus cereus. Improperly sterilized milking machines contain thermoduric micrococci, Bacillus spp. and Microbacterium spp. predominantly compared to coliforms and streptococci. Rubber hoses predominantly contribute to pseudomonads rather than thermodurics.

Water supplies

At dairy-farms, the water can be a predominant source of microbial contamination. Water used in production should be of good bacteriological quality. Inadequately or uncleaned, storage tanks, untreated water supplies from natural sources like bore wells, tanks and rivers, may also be contaminated with the faecal microbes (e.g. Coliforms, Streptococci and Clostridia). In addition, a wide variety of saprophytic bacteria (i.e. Pseudomonas, Coliforms, other Gram negative rods, Bacillus spores, Coryneform bacteria and lactic acid bacteria) may also be present in water and may contaminate the milk potentially. The warm water used for udder washing is potent source of Pseudomonas and Coliforms which may even cause mastitis.

Airborne contamination

Aerial contamination of milk by bacteria is insignificant, in comparison to microbes with those that are derived from the teat surfaces. The microbial counts of air in sheds rarely exceed 200 cfu/l. Micrococci account for >50% of the aerial microflora. Air contains dust, moisture and bacteria; hence its entry should be minimized in milk. Micrococci, Coryneforms, Bacillus spores, streptococci, and Gram negative rods are the major genera present in air. In general, more air incorporated into milk leads to the faster growth of bacteria. Following are some of the practices that increase aerial counts in milk:

- Sweeping of floors just before milking process
- Handling hay and feed shortly before milking process
- Brushing of animals prior to milking process
- Having the dusty bedding materials for animals
- Allowing dust and dirt to accumulate on the walls or ceiling of sheds

PHYSICAL METHODS-THERMAL PROCESSING

Introduction

Heat kills microorganisms by changing the physical and chemical properties of their proteins. When **heat** is used to preserve foods, the number of microorganisms present, the **microbial load** , is an important consideration. Various types of microorganisms must also be considered because different levels of resistance exist. For example, bacterial spores are much more difficult to kill than vegetative bacilli. In addition, increasing acidity enhances the killing process in food preservation.

High Temperature

Three basic heat treatments are used in food preservation: **pasteurization**, in which foods are treated at about 62°C for 30 minutes or 72°C for 15 to 17 s; **hot filling**, in which liquid foods and juices are boiled before being placed into containers; and **steam treatment** under pressure, such as used in the canning method. The heat resistance of microorganisms is usually expressed as the **thermal death time**, the time necessary at a certain temperature to kill a stated number of particular microorganisms under specified conditions.

Pasteurization

It is the process of heating a food-usually a liquid-to or below its boiling point for a defined period of time. The purpose is to destroy all pathogens, reduce the number of bacteria, inactivate enzymes and extend the shelf life of a food product. Pasteurization treatment is able to kill most heat resistant non spore forming organisms like Mycobacterium tuberculosis and Coxiella burnetti. Foods with a pH of less than 12.6, such as milk and spaghetti sauce, can be pasteurized. Permanent stabilitythat is, shelf life of about two years is obtained with foods that can withstand prolonged heating, such as bottled juices. There is a greater loss of flavour from foods that are exposed to a longer time-temperature relationship. Therefore, temporary stability (that is, limited shelf life) is only obtained with some foods where prolonged heating would destroy its quality. These foods, such as milk, usually require subsequent refrigeration. "High Temperature Short Time" (HTST) and "Ultra High Temperature" (UHT) processes have been developed to retain a food's texture and flavour quality parameters. Pasteurization is not intended to kill all microorganisms in the food. Instead pasteurization aims to reduce the number of viable pathogens so that they are unlikely to cause disease. Pasteurization involves a comparatively low order of heat treatment, generally at temperature below the boiling point of water. eating may be done by means of steam , hot water, dry heat or electric currents . Products are immediately cooled. Desired pasteurization can be achieved by a combination of time and temperature such as heating food to a low temperature and maintain for a long time i.e. LTLT -62.8°C for 30 minute , or by heating food to a high temp and maintain for a short time: HTST-71.7°C for 15 second.

Pasteurization is used when more rigorous heat treatment might harm the quality of the food product, as the market milk and for the main spoilage organisms which are not heat resistant, such as yeast in fruit juice. It also kills the pathogens .

Batch pasteurizer

Ultra heat pasteurization

In this process milk is heated to 120-138°C for 2-4 seconds and followed by rapid cooling. This treatment kills all the spoilage microorganisms. UHT pasteurized milk is packaged aseptically resulting in a shelf stable product that does not require refrigeration until opened.

Heat Resistance of Microorganisms and Their Spores

It is expressed in terms of their thermal death time (TDT).

Thermal death time (TDT)

It is the time taken to kill a given number of microorganisms or spores at a certain temperature under specified conditions.

Thermal death point

It is the temperature necessary to kill all the organisms in ten minutes.

Heat resistance of different microorganisms is different. Microorganisms are more heat resistant than their spores. Heat resistance of vegetative yeast is 50-58°C in 10-15 min and the ascospores is 60°C for 10-15 min. However, yeast and spores are killed by pasteurization.

Heat Resistance of Microorganisms

Heat resistance of mold is 60°C in 5 to 10 min and asexual spores are more heat resistance than the ordinary mycelium and require a temperature 5-10°C higher for their destruction. Aspergillus, Muco, ,Penicillium are more resistant than yeast. Heat resistance of bacteria and bacterial spores is different. Cells high in lipid content and capsule containing bacteria are harder to kill. Higher the optimal and maximal temperature for growth , the greater the resistance to killing.

Heat Resistance of Enzymes

Most of the food and microbial enzymes are destroyed at 79.4°C . Some hydrolases will retain a substantial levels of activity after an ultra high temperature treatment. Bovine phosphatase, if present, in processed milk indicates that the milk was not properly pasteurized.

D Value

It is the decimal reduction time, or the time required to destroy 90% of the organisms. Mathmatically, it is equal to reciprocal of the slop of the survivor curve and is a measure of the death rate of a microorganisms. When D is determined at 250°F, it is expressed as D_r.

D value of organisms

Z Value

It refers to the degree F required to reduce TDT tenfold. Mathematically, this value is equal to the reciprocal of the slope of the TDT curve.

F Value

This value is the equivalent time, in min at 250°F, of all heat considered, with respect to its capacity to destroy spores or vegetative cells of a particular organisms or F is the time in minute required to destroy the microorganisms in a specified medium at 250°F.

Thermal Death Time Curve

Mean viable counts determined at intervals of 5 minute are as follows-

Time Mean viable count 5 3120.0 10 65.015 19.0

Time of heating in min is plotted on semi-log paper along the linear axis and the number of survivors is plotted along the log scale to produce the TDT curve .

12-D concept: It is the time temperature process that will reduce the most heat resistant Cl. botulinum spores by 12 log cycles. Processing of food for 2.52 min at 250°C reduces Cl. botulinum spores to 1 spore in 10^{12} containers

Effect of Pasteurization

The positive effects of pasteurization are the destruction of pathogenic microorganisms to increase the safety of market milk for human consumption, improved keeping qualityandinactivation of certain naturally occurring enzymes.

The negative effects are: certain preformed products of microbial origin are not inactivated during pasteurization, e.g. Staphylococcal toxins and aflatoxins. There is small loss of native aroma particularly in case of fruit juices. In case of milk, it destroys the natural microbicidal property of milk by inactivating different natural occuring antimicrobial substances and the rennet coagulation time also increases.

Pasteurization treatment of different food

Blanching

It is a kind of pasteurization generally applied to fruits and vegetables , primarily to inactive natural food enzymes. It is a common practice when such food products are to be frozen, since frozen storage itself would not completely arrest enzyme activity. Peroxidase and catalase are the most heat resistant enzymes; the activity of these enzymes is used to evaluate the effectiveness of a blanching treatment. If both are inactivated then it can be assumed that other significant enzymes also are inactivated. The heating time depends on the type of fruit or vegetable, method of heating, the size of fruits or vegetable or the temperature of the heating medium.

For commercial blanching typical times at 212°F are given

Blanching time for different foods at 212°F

Rapid changes in colour, flavor and nutritive value occur as a result of enzyme activity. Blanching is a slight heat treatment, using hot water or steam, that is applied mostly to vegetables before canning or freezing. The main objectives of blanching are to inactivate enzymes, to remove the tissue gases, to clean the tissue, to increase the temperature of the food. Blanching is also used before canning for different reasons, because enzymes will inevitably be destroyed during canning. Blanching induces a vacuum in canned goods, and it is also used to control the fill into containers (for example, spinach).

Sterilization (Retorting)

Sterilization destroys all pathogenic and spoilage microorganisms in foods and inactivates enzymes by heating. All canned foods are sterilized in a retort (a large pressure cooker) and called commercial sterilization which indicates that no viable organisms are present. This process enables food to have a shelf life of more than two years. Foods that have a pH of more than 4.6, such as meat and most vegetables must undergo severe heating conditions to destroy all pathogens. These foods are heated under pressure to 121°C for varying times. Severe conditions are applied primarly to ensure that Clostridium botulinum spores are destroyed during processing. These spores produce the deadly botulinum toxin under anaerobic conditions (that is, where there's no oxygen). The spores are destroyed by heat or are inhibited at pH values of less than 4.6 Therefore, a food with a pH of less than 4.6 that is packaged anaerobically, such as spaghetti sauce, doesn't need to undergo such a severe heat treatment. The destruction of vegetative and sporeforming organism and pathogens is secondary objective of commercially sterilized foods.

Nicolas Appert , a Parisian confectioner by trade, established the heat processing of foods as an industry in 1810. The food product is washed, sorted, and graded and then subjected to steam for three to five minutes. This last process called blanching, destroys many enzymes in the food product and prevents further cellular metabolism. The food is then peeled and cored, and diseased portions are removed. For canning, containers are evacuated and placed in a pressurised steam steriliser, similar to an autoclave at 121°C. This removes especially Bacillus and Clostridium spores. If canning is defective, foods may become contaminated by anaerobic, bacteria which produce gas. These are species of Clostridium, and coliform bacteria (a group of Gram-negative non spore-forming rods which ferment lactose to acid and gas at 32°C in 48 hours).

Canning cooking fruits or vegetables, sealing them in sterile cans or jars, and boiling the containers to kill or weaken any remaining bacteria as a form of pasteurization. High-acid fruits like strawberries require no preservatives to can and holding for only a short boiling cycle, whereas marginal fruits such as tomatoes require longer boiling and addition of other acidic elements. Many vegetables require pressure canning. Food preserved by canning or bottling is at immediate risk of spoilage once the can or bottle has been opened. Lack of quality control in the canning process may allow ingress of water or micro-organisms. Clostridium botulinum produces an acute toxin within the food and may lead to severe illness or death. This organism produces no gas or obvious taste and remains undetected by taste or smell. Food contaminated in this way include Corn, beef and Tuna.

In canning process heat is applied to food that is sealed in a jar in order to destroy any microorganisms that can cause food spoilage. Proper canning techniques stop this spoilage by heating the food for a specific period of time and killing these unwanted microorganisms. During the canning process, air is driven from the jar and a vacuum is formed as the jar cools and seals.

Water-bath canning and pressure canning are two approved methods of canning.

Water-Bath Canning

This method sometimes referred to as hot water canning, uses a large kettle of boiling water (Figure 12.4). Filled jars are submerged in the water and heated to an internal temperature of 212°F for a specific period of time. This method is used for processing high-acid foods, such as fruit, items made from fruit, pickles, pickled food, and tomatoes.

Pressure Canning

Pressure canning uses a large kettle that produces steam in a locked compartment (Figure 12.5). The filled jars in the kettle reach an internal temperature of -240 °C under a specific pressure (stated in pounds) that is measured with a dial gauge or weighted gauge on the pressure-canner cover. A pressure canner should be used for processing vegetables and other low-acid foods, such as meat, poultry and fish.

Drying

One of the oldest methods of food preservation is by drying, which reduces water activity sufficiently to delay or prevent bacterial growth. Drying is done to produce concentrated form of foods, inhibits microbial growth and autolytic enzymes, retains most nutrients. Drying can cause loss of some nutrients, particularly thiamine and vitamin C. Sulphur dioxide is sometimes added to dried fruits to retain vitamin C, but some individuals are sensitive to this substance.

Most types of meat can be dried. This is especially valuable in the case of pig meat, since it is difficult to keep without preservation. Many fruits can also be dried; for example, the process is often applied to apples, pears, bananas, mangos, papaya, and coconut and grapes . Drying is also the normal means of preservation for cereal grains such as wheat, maize, oats, barley, rice, millet and rye. Drying is an excellent way of preserving several of the seasonal fruits for use during the off season. There are several types of dryers which are used. These include: drum dryer, cabinet dryer, tunnel dryer, rotary dryer, spray dryer and solar dryer. The basic methods of drying involves ai r and contac t dr ying under atmospheric pressure . In this cas e the heat is transferred through the food either from heated air or heated surfaces, and the resulting water vapour is removed with the air current . Solar drying, sun drying, drum and spray drying all use this technique.

Advantages of drying are many

i) Long Shelf Life – Since most microorganisms responsible for food spoilage are unable to grow and multiply in the absence of moisture, spoilage due to microbial degradation is limited in dried foods. Furthermore, enzymes which catalyse undesirable changes in foods need moisture to be effective.

ii) Reduced Weight – This results in reduced transportation, storage and shipping costs.

iii) Convenience – The production of convenience items with novelty appeal for niche markets makes drying an attractive option.

iv) Concentration of nutrients – The removal of most of the water from a food results in a highly concentrated source of nutrients.

v) No refrigeration is required for dried products – Savings in energy and storage costs together with the long shelf life provide a lucrative processing alternative for tropical countries.

Disadvantages of Drying

Disadvantages of Drying are few and mainly relate to oxidation, which usually accompanies drying. This results in losses of micronutrients such as carotene and ascorbic acid and minimal loss in protein as a result of browning reactions. Reduced consumer appeal is often linked with the latter. There might also be changes in flavour and texture if drying is not properly controlled, particularly with regard to maximum temperatures.

Microwave Sterilization

Microwave sterilization is a thermal process. A microwave oven works by passing non ionizing microwave radiation, usually at a frequency of 2.125 GHz (a wavelength of 12.212 cm), through the food. Microwave radiation is between common radio and infrared frequencies. Microwave heating takes place due to the polarization effect of electromagnetic radiation at frequencies between 300 MHz and 300 GHz. It delivers energy to the food package under pressure and controlled temperature to achieve inactivation of bacteria harmful for humans. Most processed foods today are heat treated to kill bacteria. Prolong exposure to high heat often diminishes product quality. Microwaves interact with polar water molecules and charged ions. The friction resulting from molecules aligning in rapidly alternating electromagnetic field generates the heat within food. Since the heat is produced directly in the food, the thermal processing time is sharply reduced. The colour, texture and other sensory attributes of foods processed by microwave sterilization are often better compared with those of conventionally retorted foods while meeting microbial safety requirements. US Federal Communication Commission (FCC) allocates 915 MHz and 21250 MHz bands for industrial and domestic microwave heating applications. The microwave sterilization technology using the combination of 915 MHz microwave and conventional heating to improve heating uniformity. Microwave ovens use electromagnetic radiation to excite water molecules in food. The actual waves penetrate only about 10 inches from the source of the radiation. Within the food, the waves only penetrate 3/12 to 1 inch on all sides. As a result, the actual ovens must be limited in size. Heat is produced within the food by the friction of water molecules, which spreads to the centre of the food by conduction. Small portions are cooked rapidly in microwave ovens. As the quantity of food increases, however, the efficiency is lost.

Microwave heating has also found applications in the food industry, including tempering of frozen foods for further processing, pre-cooking of bacon for institutional use and final drying of pasta products. In those applications, microwave heating demonstrates significant advantages over conventional methods in reducing process time and improving food quality.

The shelf life of a product is determined by its microbiological safety and sensory attributes. In general, microwave sterilization can achieve the same reduction of bacterial population as conventional retorting. Products intended for microwave sterilization are usually packaged in plastic trays or pouches. The ability of plastics to withstand oxygen permeation will affect the organoleptic or sensory acceptance of the product during storage. Normal shelf life expectancy of microwave-sterilized products pre-packaged in plastic containers or pouches is 2-3 years or longer. With innovative plastic technologies coming to the market, the new generations of plastics may increase the expected shelf life even longer.

IV

Food – Borne Infection & Diseases

Food – borne infection & diseases: food poisoning by micro – organism. Food intoxication: Botulism – Organism, toxin, foods involved, diseases caused. Prevention of outbreaks. Food infection: Salmonellosis – source of salmonella, foods involved, prevention of outbreaks.

Causes of Food Poisoning

Many different disease-causing germs can contaminate foods, so there are many different foodborne infections (also called foodborne disease or food poisoning).

- Researchers have identified more than 250 foodborne diseases.
- Most of them are infections, caused by a variety of bacteria, viruses, and parasites.
- Harmful toxins and chemicals also can contaminate foods and cause foodborne illness.

CDC estimates that each year 48 million people get sick from a foodborne illness, 128,000 are hospitalized, and 3,000 die.

Do I Have Food Poisoning?

Common symptoms of foodborne diseases are nausea, vomiting, stomach cramps, and diarrhea. However, symptoms may differ among the different types of foodborne diseases. Symptoms can sometimes be severe, and some foodborne illnesses can even be life-threatening. Although anyone can get a foodborne illness, some people are more likely to develop one. Those groups include:

- Older adults
- Young children
- People with immune systems weakened from medical conditions, such as diabetes, liver disease, kidney disease, organ transplants, or HIV/AIDS, or from receiving chemotherapy or radiation treatment.
- Pregnant women

Most people with a foodborne illness get better without medical treatment, but people with severe symptoms should see their doctor.

Learn more about the symptoms and sources of food poisoning >>

Some Common Foodborne Germs

The top five germs that cause illnesses from food eaten in the United States are:

- Norovirus
- Salmonella
- Clostridium perfringens
- Campylobacter
- Staphylococcus aureus (Staph)

Some other germs don't cause as many illnesses, but when they do, the illnesses are more likely to lead to hospitalization. Those germs include:

E. coli

- Clostridium botulinum (botulism)
- Listeria
- Escherichia coli (E. coli)
- Vibrio

Food Technology & Processing

Bacterial Food Poisoning

Al B. Wagner, Jr., Professor and Extension Food Technologist

Food borne illness is an ever-present threat that can be prevented with proper care and handling of food products. It is estimated that between 24 and 81 million cases of food borne diarrhea disease occur each year in the United States, costing between $5 billion and $17 billion in medical care and lost productivity.

Chemicals, heavy metals, parasites, fungi, viruses and bacteria can cause food borne illness. Bacteria related food poisoning is the most common, but fewer than 20 of the many thousands of different bacteria actually are the culprits. More than 90 percent of the cases of food poisoning each year are caused by Staphylococcus aureus, Salmonella, Clostridium perfringens, Campylobacter, Listeria monocytogenes, Vibrio parahaemolyticus, Bacillus cereus, and Entero-pathogenic Escherichia coli. These bacteria are commonly found on many raw foods. Normally a large number of food-poisoning bacteria must be present to cause illness. Therefore, illness can be prevented by (1) controlling the initial number of bacteria present, (2) preventing the small number from growing, (3) destroying the bacteria by proper cooking and (4) avoiding re-contamination.

Poor personal hygiene, improper cleaning of storage and preparation areas and unclean utensils cause contamination of raw and cooked foods. Mishandling of raw and cooked foods allows bacteria to grow. The temperature range in which most bacteria grow is between 40 degrees F (5 degrees C) and 140 degrees F (60 degrees C). Raw and cooked foods should not be kept in this danger zone any longer than absolutely necessary. Undercooking or improper processing of home-canned foods can cause very serious food poisoning.

Since food-poisoning bacteria are often present on many foods, knowing the characteristics of such bacteria is essential to an effective control program.

Staphylococcus aureus

Man's respiratory passages, skin and superficial wounds are common sources of S. aureus. When S. aureus is allowed to grow in foods, it can produce a toxin that causes illness. Although cooking destroys the bacteria, the toxin produced is heat stable and may not be destroyed. Staphylococcal food poisoning occurs most often in foods that require hand preparation, such as potato salad, ham salad and sandwich spreads. Sometimes these types of foods are left at room temperature for long periods of time, allowing the bacteria to grow and produce toxin. Good personal hygiene while handling foods will help keep S. aureus out of foods, and refrigeration of raw and cooked foods will prevent the growth of these bacteria if any are present.

Salmonella

The gastrointestinal tracts of animals and man are common sources of Salmonella. High protein foods such as meat, poultry, fish and eggs are most commonly associated with Salmonella. However, any food that becomes contaminated and is then held at improper temperatures can cause salmonellosis. Salmonella are destroyed at cooking temperatures above 150 degrees F. The major causes of salmonellosis are contamination of cooked foods and insufficient cooking. Contamination of cooked foods occurs from contact with surfaces or utensils that were not properly washed after use with raw products. If Salmonella is present on raw or cooked foods, its growth can be controlled by refrigeration below 40 degrees F.

Clostridium perfringens

C. perfringens is found in soil, dust and the gastrointestinal tracts of animals and man. When food containing a large number of C. perfringens is consumed, the bacteria produce a toxin in the intestinal tract that causes illness. C. perfringens can exist as a heat-resistant spore, so it may survive cooking and grow to large numbers if the cooked food is held between 40 degrees F and 140 degrees F for an extensive time period. Meat and poultry dishes, sauces and gravies are the foods most frequently involved. Hot foods should be served immediately or held above 140 degrees F. When refrigerating large volumes of gravies, meat dishes, etc., divide them into small portions so they will cool rapidly. The food should be reheated to 165° F. prior to serving.

Clostridium botulinum

Botulism accounts for fewer than one of every 400 cases of food poisoning in the U.S., but two factors make it very important. First, it has caused death in approximately 30 percent of the cases; and secondly, it occurs mostly in home-canned foods. In 1975, for example, 18 or 19 confirmed cases of botulism were caused by home-processed foods, and the other was caused by a commercial product that was mishandled in the home. Cl. botulinum can exist as a heat-resistant spore, and can grow and produce a neurotoxin in under processed, home-canned foods. An affected food may show signs of spoilage such as a bulging can or an off-odor. This is not true in all cases, so canned foods should not be tasted before heating. The botulinum toxin is destroyed by boiling the food for 10 minutes.

Vibrio parahaemolyticus

V. parahaemolyticus is found on seafood's, and requires the salt environment of sea water for growth. V. parahaemolyticus is very sensitive to cold and heat. Proper storage of perishable seafood's below 40 degrees F, and subsequent cooking and holding above 140 degrees F, will destroy all the V. parahaemolyticus on seafood's. Food poisoning caused by this bacterium is a result of insufficient cooking and/or contamination of the cooked product by a raw product, followed by improper storage temperature. It is a major problem in Japan where many seafood's are consumed raw. Vibrio vulnificus is another member of the vibrio genus that is found in the marine environment. V. vulnificus is truly an emerging pathogen, but it can be controlled with proper cooking and refrigeration.

Bacillus cereus

B. cereus is found in dust, soil and spices. It can survive normal cooking as a heat-resistant spore, and then produce a large number of cells if the storage temperature is incorrect. Starchy foods such as rice, macaroni and potato dishes are most often involved. The spores may be present on raw foods, and their ability to survive high cooking temperatures requires that cooked foods be served hot or cooled rapidly to prevent the growth of this bacteria.

Listeria

Before the 1980's most problems associated with disease caused by Listeria were related to cattle or sheep. This changed with food related outbreaks in Nova Scotia, Massachusetts, California and Texas. As a result of its widespread distribution in the environment, its ability to survive long periods of time under adverse conditions, and its ability to grow at refrigeration temperatures, Listeria is now recognized as an important food-borne pathogen.

Immunocompromised humans such as pregnant women or the elderly are highly susceptible to virulent Listeria. Listeria monocytogenes is the most consistently pathogenic species causing listeriosis. In humans, ingestion of the bacteria may be marked by a flu-like illness or symptoms may be so mild that they go unnoticed. A carrier state can develop. Death is rare in healthy adults; however, the mortality rate may approximate 30 percent in the immunocompromised, new born or very young.

As mentioned earlier Listeria monocytogenes is a special problem since it can survive adverse conditions. It can grow in a pH range of 5.0-9.5 in good growth medium. The organism has survived the pH 5 environment of cottage cheese and ripening cheddar. It is salt tolerant surviving concentrations as high as 30.5 percent for 100 days at 39.2 degrees F, but only 5 days if held at 98.6 degrees F.

The key point is that refrigeration temperatures don not stop growth of Listeria. It is capable of doubling in numbers every 1.5 days at 39.5 degrees F. Since high heat, greater than 170 degrees F, will inactivate the Listeria organisms, post-process contamination from environmental sources then becomes a critical control point for many foods. Since Listeria will grow slowly at refrigeration temperatures, product rotation becomes even more important.

Yersinia enterocolitica

Even though Yersinia enterocolitica is not a frequent cause of human infection in the U.S., it is often involved in illness with very severe symptoms. Yersiniosis, infection caused by this microorganism, occurs most commonly in the form of gastroenteritis. Children are most severely affected. Symptoms of pseudoappendicitis has resulted in many unnecessary appendectomies. Death is rare and recovery is generally complete in 1-2 days. Arthritis has been identified as an infrequent but significant sequel of this infection.

Y. enterocolitica is commonly present in foods but with the exception of pork, most isolates do not cause disease. Like Listeria this organism is also one that can grow at refrigeration temperatures. It is sensitive to heat (5%) and acidity (pH 4.6), and will normally be inactivated by environmental conditions that will kill Salmonellae.

Campylobacter jejuni

C. jejuni was first isolated from human diarrhea stools in 1971. Since then it has continually gained recognition as a disease causing organism in humans.

C. jejuni enteritis is primarily transferred from animal origin foods to humans in developed countries. However, fecal contamination of food and water and contact with sick people or animals, predominates in developing countries.

Although milk has been most frequently identified throughout the world to be a vehicle for Campylobacter, one anticipates that future investigations will identify poultry and its products and meats (beef, pork, and lamb) as major reservoirs and vehicles.

C. jejuni dies off rapidly at ambient temperature and atmosphere, and grows poorly in food.

The principles of animal science will play a significant role in the control of this ubiquitous organism. Hygienic slaughter and processing procedures will preclude cross-contamination while adequate cooling and aeration will cause a decrease in the microbial load. In addition, thorough cooking of meat and poultry products followed by proper storage should assist in maintaining food integrity and less contamination.

Enteropathogenic Escherichia coli

Enteropathoginec E. coli is a significant cause of diarrhea in developing countries and localities of poor sanitation. In the U.S. it has been associated with “travelers’ diarrhea.” However the latest outbreak in North America occurred in a nursing home in Ontario. This was a severe outbreak of E. coli0157:H7 associated hemorrhagic colitis.

There are at least four subgroups of enteropathogenic E. coli: enterotoxigenic, enterinvasive, hemorrhagic, and enteropathogenic. Each strain has different characteristics.

The major source of the bacteria in the environment is probably the feces of infected humans, but there may also be animal reservoirs. Feces and untreated water are the most likely sources for contamination of food.

Control of enteropathogenic E. coli and other food-borne pathogens such as Salmonella and Staphylococcus aureus can be achieved. Precautions should include adequate cooking and avoidance of recontamination of cooked meat by contaminated equipment, water or infected food handlers. Food service establishments should monitor adequacy of cooking, holding times, and temperatures as well as the personal hygiene of food handlers.

Prevention

The first step in preventing food poisoning is to assume that all foods may cause food-borne illness. Follow these steps to prevent food poisoning:

1. Wash hands, food preparation surfaces and utensils thoroughly before and after handling raw foods to prevent recontamination of cooked foods.
2. Keep refrigerated foods below 40 degrees F.
3. Serve hot foods immediately or keep them heated above 140 degrees F.

4. Divide large volumes of food into small portions for rapid cooling in the refrigerator. Hot, bulky foods in the refrigerator can raise the temperature of foods already cooled.
5. Remember the danger zone is between 40 degrees F and 140 degrees F.
6. Follow approved home-canning procedures. These can be obtained from the Extension Service or from USDA bulletins.
7. Heat canned foods thoroughly before tasting.
8. When in doubt, throw it out

Infants, older persons, women who are pregnant and anyone with a compromised immune system are especially susceptible to food-borne illness. These people should never consume raw fish, raw seafood, or raw meat type products.

You are the key to preventing food-borne illness. By observing the simple rules of good handling, food poisoning can be eliminated.

Bacteria Responsible

Description

Habitat

Types of Foods

Symptoms

Cause

Temperture Sensitivity

Staphylococcus aureus

Produces a heat-stable toxin

Nose and throat of 30 to 50 percent of healthy population; also skin and superficial wounds.

Meat and seafood salads, sandwich spreads and high salt foods.

Nausea, vomiting and diarrhea within 4 to 6 hours. No fever.

Poor personal hygiene and subsequent temperature abuse.

No growth below 40° F. Bacteria are destroyed by normal cooking but toxin is heat-stable.

Salmonella

Produces an intestinal infection

Intestinal tracts of animals and man

High protein foods – meat, poultry, fish and eggs.

Diarrhea nausea, chills, vomiting and fever within 12 to 24 hours.

Contamination of ready-to-eat foods, insufficient cooking and recontamination of cooked foods.

No growth below 40° F. Bacteria are destroyed by normal cooking.

Clostridium perfringens

Produces a spore and prefers low oxygen atmosphere. Live cells must be ingested.

Dust, soil and gastrointestinal tracts of animals and man.

Meat and poultry dishes, sauces and gravies.

Cramps and diarrhea within 12 to 24 hours. No vomiting or fever.

Improper temperature control of hot foods, and recontamination.

No growth below 40 degrees F. Bacteria are killed by normal cooking but a heat-stable spore can survive.

Clostridium botulinum

Produces a spore and requires a low oxygen atmosphere. Produces a heat-sensitive toxin.

Soils, plants, marine sediments and fish.

Home-canned foods.

Blurred vision, respiratory distress and possible DEATH.

Improper methods of home-processing foods.

Type E and Type B can grow at 38° F. Bacteria destroyed by cooking and the toxin is destroyed by boiling for 5 to 10 minutes. Heat-resistant spore can survive.

Vibrio parahaemolyticus

Requires salt for growth.

Fish and shellfish

Raw and cooked seafood.

Diarrhea, cramps, vomiting, headache and fever within 12 to 24 hours.

Recontamination of cooked foods or eating raw seafood.

No growth below 40° F. Bacteria killed by normal cooking.

Bacillus cereus

Produces a spore and grows in normal oxygen atmosphere.

Soil, dust and spices.

Starchy food.

Mild case of diarrhea and some nausea within 12 to 24 hours.

Improper holding and storage temperatures after cooking.

No growth below 40° F. Bacteria killed by normal cooking, but heat-resistant spore can survive.

Listeria monocytogenes

Survives adverse conditions for long time periods.

Soil, vegetation and water. Can survive for long periods in soil and plant materials.

Milk, soft cheeses, vegetables fertilized with manure.

Mimics meningitis. Immuno-compromised individuals most susceptible.

Contaminated raw products.

Grows at refrigeration (38-40° F) temperatures. May survive minimum pasturization tempertures (161° F for 15 seconds.)

Campylobacter jejuni

Oxygen sensitive, does not grow below 86° F.

Animal reservoirs and foods of animal origin.

Meat, poulty, milk, and mushrooms.

Diarrhea, abdomianl cramps and nausea.

Improper pasteuriztion or cooking. Cross-contamination.

Sensitive to drying or freezing. Survives in milk and water at 39° F for several weeks.

Versinia enterocolitica

Not frequent cause of human infection.

Poultry, beef, swine. Isolated only in human pathogen.

Milk, tofu, and pork.

Diarrhea, abdominal pain, vomiting. Mimics appendicitis.

Improper cooking. Cross-contamination.

Grows at refrigeration temperatures (35-40° F) Sensitive to heat (122° F)

Enteropathogenic E. coli

Can produce toxins that are heat stable and others that are heat-sensitive.

Feces of infected humans.

Meat and cheeses.

Diarrhea, abdominal cramps, no fever.

Inadequate cooking. Recontamination of cooked product.

Organisms can be controlled by heating. Can grow at refrigeration temperatures.

Food Intoxication

It refers to the consumption of toxic chemicals liberated or produced by bacterial growth in food. These respective toxins results in variety of illness of the consumers. These toxins are not visible to naked eye but will change the chemical properties of the food.

About Botulism

This illustration depicts a three-dimensional (3D) computer-generated image of a group of anaerobic, spore-forming, Clostridium sp. organisms.

Botulism ("BOT-choo-liz-um") is a rare but serious illness caused by a toxin that attacks the body's nerves and causes difficulty breathing, muscle paralysis, and even death. This toxin is made by Clostridium botulinum and sometimes Clostridium butyricum and Clostridium baratii bacteria. These bacteria can produce the toxin in food, wounds, and the intestines of infants.

The bacteria that make botulinum toxin are found naturally in many places, but it's rare for them to make people sick. These bacteria make spores, which act like protective coatings. Spores help the bacteria survive in the environment, even in extreme conditions. The spores usually do not cause people to become sick, even when they're eaten. But under certain conditions, these spores can grow and make one of the most lethal toxins known. The conditions in which the spores can grow and make toxin are:

- Low-oxygen or no oxygen (anaerobic) environment
- Low acid

- Low sugar
- Low salt
- A certain temperature range
- A certain amount of water

For example, improperly home canned , preserved , or fermented food 's can provide the right conditions for spores to grow and make botulinum toxin. When people eat these foods, they can become seriously ill, or even die, if they don't get proper medical treatment quickly.

toxin

Botulinum toxin, one of the most poisonous biological substances known, is a neurotoxin produced by the bacterium Clostridium botulinum. C. botulinum elaborates eight antigenically distinguishable exotoxins (A, B, C1, C2, D, E, F and G). All serotypes interfere with neural transmission by blocking the release of acetylcholine, the principal neurotransmitter at the neuromuscular junction, causing muscle paralysis. The weakness induced by injection with botulinum toxin A usually lasts about three months. Botulinum toxins now play a very significant role in the management of a wide variety of medical conditions, especially strabismus and focal dystonias, hemifacial spasm, and various spastic movement disorders, headaches, hypersalivation, hyperhidrosis, and some chronic conditions that respond only partially to medical treatment. The list of possible new indications is rapidly expanding. The cosmetological applications include correction of lines, creases and wrinkling all over the face, chin, neck, and chest to dermatological applications such as hyperhidrosis. Injections with botulinum toxin are generally well tolerated and side effects are few. A precise knowledge and understanding of the functional anatomy of the mimetic muscles is absolutely necessary to correctly use botulinum toxins in clinical practice.

Foodborne botulism is a serious, potentially fatal disease. However, it is relatively rare. It is an intoxication usually caused by ingestion of potent neurotoxins, the botulinum toxins, formed in contaminated foods. Person to person transmission of botulism does not occur.

Spores produced by the bacteria Clostridium botulinum are heat-resistant and exist widely in the environment, and in the absence of oxygen they germinate, grow and then excrete toxins. There are 7 distinct forms of botulinum toxin, types A–G. Four of these (types A, B, E and rarely F) cause human botulism. Types C, D and E cause illness in other mammals, birds and fish.

Botulinum toxins are ingested through improperly processed food in which the bacteria or the spores survive, then grow and produce the toxins. Though mainly a foodborne intoxication, human botulism can also be caused by intestinal infection with C. botulinum in infants, wound infections, and by inhalation.

Symptoms of foodborne botulism

Botulinum toxins are neurotoxic and therefore affect the nervous system. Foodborne botulism is characterized by descending, flaccid paralysis that can cause respiratory failure. Early symptoms include marked fatigue, weakness and vertigo, usually followed by blurred vision, dry mouth and difficulty in swallowing and speaking. Vomiting, diarrhoea, constipation and abdominal swelling may also occur. The disease can progress to weakness in the neck and arms, after which the respiratory muscles and muscles of the lower body are affected. There is no fever and no loss of consciousness.

The symptoms are not caused by the bacterium itself, but by the toxin produced by the bacterium. Symptoms usually appear within 12 to 36 hours (within a minimum and maximum range of 4 hours to 8 days) after exposure. Incidence of botulism is low, but the mortality rate is high if prompt diagnosis and appropriate, immediate treatment (early administration of antitoxin and intensive respiratory care) are not given. The disease can be fatal in 5 to 10% of cases.

Exposure and transmission

Foodborne botulism

C. botulinum is an anaerobic bacterium, meaning it can only grow in the absence of oxygen. Foodborne botulism occurs when C. botulinum grows and produces toxins in food prior to consumption. C. botulinum produces spores and they exist widely in the environment including soil, river and sea water.

The growth of the bacteria and the formation of toxin occur in products with low oxygen content and certain combinations of storage temperature and preservative parameters. This happens most often in lightly preserved foods and in inadequately processed, home-canned or home-bottled foods.

C. botulinum will not grow in acidic conditions (pH less than 4.6), and therefore the toxin will not be formed in acidic foods (however, a low pH will not degrade any pre-formed toxin). Combinations of low storage temperature and salt contents and/or pH are also used to prevent the growth of the bacteria or the formation of the toxin.

The botulinum toxin has been found in a variety of foods, including low-acid preserved vegetables, such as green beans, spinach, mushrooms, and beets; fish, including canned tuna, fermented, salted and smoked fish; and meat products, such as ham and sausage. The food implicated differs between countries and reflects local eating habits and food preservation procedures. Occasionally, commercially prepared foods are involved.

Though spores of C. botulinum are heat-resistant, the toxin produced by bacteria growing out of the spores under anaerobic conditions is destroyed by boiling (for example, at internal temperature greater than 85 °C for 5 minutes or longer). Therefore, ready-to-eat foods in low oxygen-packaging are more frequently involved in cases of foodborne botulism.

Food samples associated with suspect cases must be obtained immediately, stored in properly sealed containers, and sent to laboratories in order to identify the cause and to prevent further cases.

Infant botulism

Infant botulism occurs mostly in infants under 6 months of age. Different from foodborne botulism caused by ingestion of pre-formed toxins in food, it occurs when infants ingest C. botulinum spores, which germinate into bacteria that colonize in the gut and release toxins. In most adults and children older than about 6 months, this would not happen because natural defences in intestines that develop over time prevent germination and growth of the bacterium.

C. botulinum in infants include constipation, loss of appetite, weakness, an altered cry and a striking loss of head control. Although there are several possible sources of infection for infant botulism, spore-contaminated honey has been associated with a number of cases. Parents and caregivers are therefore warned not to feed honey to the infants before the age of 1 year.

Wound botulism

Wound botulism is rare and occurs when the spores get into an open wound and are able to reproduce in an anaerobic environment. The symptoms are similar to the foodborne botulism, but may take up to 2 weeks to appear. This form of the disease has been associated with substance abuse, particularly when injecting black tar heroin.

Inhalation botulism

Inhalation botulism is rare and does not occur naturally, for example it is associated with accidental or intentional events (such as bioterrorism) which result in release of the toxins in aerosols. Inhalation botulism exhibits a similar clinical footprint to foodborne botulism. The median lethal dose for humans has been estimated at 2 nanograms of botulinum toxin per kilogram of bodyweight, which is approximately 3 times greater than in foodborne cases.

Following inhalation of the toxin, symptoms become visible between 1–3 days, with longer onset times for lower levels of intoxication. Symptoms proceed in a similar manner to ingestion of botulinum toxin and culminate in muscular paralysis and respiratory failure.

If exposure to the toxin via aerosol inhalation is suspected, additional exposure to the patient and others must be prevented.

The patient's clothing must be removed and stored in plastic bags until it can be washed thoroughly with soap and water. The patient should shower and be decontaminated immediately.

Other types of intoxication

Waterborne botulism could theoretically result from the ingestion of the pre-formed toxin. However, as common water treatment processes (such as boiling, disinfection with 0.1% hypochlorite bleach solution) destroy the toxin, the risk is considered low.

Botulism of undetermined origin usually involves adult cases where no food or wound source can be identified. These cases are comparable to infant botulism and may occur when the normal gut flora has been altered as a result of surgical procedures or antibiotic therapy.

Adverse effects of the pure toxin have been reported as a result of its medical and/or cosmetic use in patients, see more on 'Botox' below.

'Botox'

The bacterium C. botulinum is the same bacterium that is used to produce Botox, a pharmaceutical product predominantly injected for clinical and cosmetic use. Botox treatments employ the purified and heavily diluted botulinum neurotoxin type A. Treatment is administered in the medical setting, tailored according to the needs of the patient and is usually well tolerated although occasional side effects are observed.

Diagnosis and treatment

Diagnosis is usually based on clinical history and clinical examination followed by laboratory confirmation including demonstrating the presence of botulinum toxin in serum, stool or food, or a culture of C. botulinum from stool, wound or food. Misdiagnosis of botulism sometimes occurs as it is often confused with stroke, Guillain-Barré syndrome, or myasthenia gravis.

Antitoxin should be administered as soon as possible after a clinical diagnosis. Early administration is effective in reducing mortality rates. Severe botulism cases require supportive treatment, especially mechanical ventilation, which may be required for weeks or even months. Antibiotics are not required (except in the case of wound botulism). A vaccine against botulism exists but it is rarely used as its effectiveness has not been fully evaluated and it has demonstrated negative side effects.

Prevention

Prevention of foodborne botulism is based on good practice in food preparation particularly during heating/sterilization and hygiene. Foodborne botulism may be prevented by the inactivation of the bacterium and its spores in heat-sterilized (for example, retorted) or canned products or by inhibiting bacterial growth and toxin production in other products. The vegetative forms of bacteria can be destroyed by boiling but the spores can remain viable after boiling even for several hours. However, the spores can be killed by very high temperature treatments such as commercial canning.

Commercial heat pasteurization (including vacuum packed pasteurized products and hot smoked products) may not be sufficient to kill all spores and therefore the safety of these products must be based on preventing bacterial growth and toxin production. Refrigeration temperatures combined with salt content and/or acidic conditions will prevent the growth of the bacteria and formation of toxin.

The WHO Five Keys to Safer Food serve as the basis for educational programmes to train food handlers and educate the consumers. They are especially important in preventing food poisoning.

The Five Keys are:

- keep clean
- separate raw and cooked
- cook thoroughly
- keep food at safe temperatures
- use safe water and raw materials.

WHO's response

Botulism outbreaks are rare but are public health emergencies that require rapid recognition to identify the disease source, distinguish outbreak types (between natural, accidental or potentially deliberate), prevent additional cases and effectively administer treatment to affected patients.

Successful treatment depends significantly on early diagnosis and the rapid administration of the botulinum antitoxin.

WHO's role in responding to outbreaks of botulism that may be of international concern is as follows.

Surveillance and detection: WHO supports the strengthening of national surveillance and international alert systems to ensure rapid local outbreak detection and an efficient international response. WHO's main tool for these activities of surveillance, coordination and response is the use of the International Network of Food Safety Authorities (INFOSAN) which links national authorities in Member States in charge of managing food safety events. This network is managed jointly by FAO and WHO.

Risk assessment: WHO response is based on a risk assessment methodology that includes consideration of whether the outbreak is natural, accidental, or, possibly, intentional. WHO also provides scientific assessments as basis for international food safety standards, guidelines and recommendations developed by the Codex Alimentarius Commission.

Containment at the disease source: WHO coordinates with national and local authorities in order to contain outbreaks at their source.

Botulism is a rare but serious condition caused by a toxin that attacks the body's nerves. Botulism may cause life-threatening symptoms. A type of bacteria called Clostridium botulinum produces the toxin. Botulism can occur as the result of food or wound contamination. The condition can also occur when bacterial spores grow in the intestines of infants. In rare cases, botulism can also be caused by medical treatment or bioterrorism.

Three common forms of botulism are:

- **Foodborne botulism.** The harmful bacteria thrive and make the toxin in environments with little oxygen, such as in home-canned food.
- **Wound botulism.** If these bacteria get into a cut, they can cause a dangerous infection that makes the toxin.
- **Infant botulism.** This most generic form of botulism begins after spores of C. botulinum bacteria grow in a baby's intestinal tract. It typically occurs in babies between the ages of 2 months and 8 months. In rare cases, this form of intestinal botulism also affects adults.

Occasionally, botulism happens when too much botulinum toxin is injected for cosmetic or medical reasons. This rare form is called iatrogenic botulism. The term "iatrogenic" means an illness caused by medical exam or treatment.

Another rare form of botulism can occur from inhaling toxins. This may happen as the result of bioterrorism.

All forms of botulism can be fatal and are considered medical emergencies.

Symptoms

Foodborne botulism

Symptoms of foodborne botulism typically begin 12 to 36 hours after the toxin gets into your body. But depending on how much toxin you consumed, the start of symptoms may range from a few hours to a few days.

Symptoms of foodborne botulism include:

- Trouble swallowing or speaking
- Dry mouth
- Facial weakness on both sides of the face
- Blurred or double vision
- Drooping eyelids
- Trouble breathing
- Nausea, vomiting and stomach cramps
- Paralysis

Wound botulism

Symptoms of wound botulism appear about 10 days after the toxin enters your body. Wound botulism symptoms include:

- Trouble swallowing or speaking
- Facial weakness on both sides of the face
- Blurred or double vision
- Drooping eyelids
- Trouble breathing
- Paralysis

The area around the wound may not always appear swollen and show a change of color.

Infant botulism

Problems generally begin 18 to 36 hours after the toxin enters the baby's body. Symptoms include:

- Constipation, which is often the first symptom
- Floppy movements due to muscle weakness and trouble controlling the head
- Weak cry
- Irritability
- Drooling
- Drooping eyelids
- Tiredness
- Trouble sucking or feeding
- Paralysis

Certain symptoms don't typically occur with botulism. For example, botulism doesn't usually raise blood pressure or heart rate or cause fever or confusion. Sometimes, though, wound botulism may cause fever.

Iatrogenic botulism

In iatrogenic botulism — when the toxin is injected for cosmetic or medical reasons — there have been rare occurrences of serious side effects. These may include headache, facial paralysis, and muscle weakness.

When to see a doctor

Seek urgent medical care if you suspect that you have botulism. Initial treatment increases your survival chances and lowers your risk of complications.

Getting medical care quickly can also alert public health officials about episodes of foodborne botulism. They may be able to keep other people from eating contaminated food. Keep in mind, though, that botulism can't spread from person to person.

An unusual cluster of botulism — especially in people with no clear link — that develops in about 12 to 48 hours may raise suspicion of bioterrorism.

Request an Appointment at Mayo Clinic

Causes

Foodborne botulism

The typical source of foodborne botulism is homemade food that is improperly canned or preserved. These foods are typically fruits, vegetables, and fish. Other foods, such as spicy peppers (chiles), foil-wrapped baked potatoes and oil infused with garlic, may also be sources of botulism.

Wound botulism

When C. botulinum bacteria get into a wound, they can multiply and make toxin. The wound may be a cut that wasn't noticed. Or the wound may be caused by a traumatic injury or surgery.

Wound botulism has increased in recent decades in people who inject heroin, which can contain spores of the bacteria. In fact, this form of botulism is more common in people who inject black tar heroin.

Infant botulism

Babies get infant botulism when the bacteria spores get into their intestines and make toxin. In some cases, the source of infant botulism may be honey. But it's more likely to be exposure to soil contaminated with the bacteria. In rare cases, this form of intestinal botulism also affects adults.

Iatrogenic botulism

Rarely, botulism happens when too much botulinum toxin is injected for cosmetic reasons, such as removing wrinkles, or for medical reasons, such as treating migraines.

Complications

Because it affects muscle control throughout your body, botulinum toxin can cause many complications. The most immediate danger is that you won't be able to breathe. Being unable to breathe is a common cause of death in botulism. Other complications, which may need rehabilitation, may include:

- Difficulty speaking
- Trouble swallowing
- Long-lasting weakness
- Shortness of breath

Prevention

Foodborne botulism

Use proper techniques when canning or preserving foods at home to make sure botulism germs are destroyed. It's also important to prepare and store food safely:

- Pressure-cook home-canned foods at 250 degrees Fahrenheit (121 Celsius) for 20 to 100 minutes, depending on the food.
- Think about boiling these foods for 10 minutes before serving them.
- Don't eat preserved food if its container is bulging or if the food smells bad. But, taste and smell won't always give away the presence of C. botulinum. Some strains don't make food smell bad or taste unusual.
- If you wrap potatoes in foil before baking, eat them hot. Loosen the foil and store the potatoes in the refrigerator — not at room temperature.
- Store homemade oils infused with garlic or herbs in the refrigerator. Throw them out after four days.

- Refrigerate canned foods after you open them.

Wound botulism

To prevent wound botulism and other serious bloodborne diseases, never inject or inhale street drugs. Keep wounds clean to prevent infection. If you think a wound is infected, seek medical treatment right away.

Infant botulism

To lower the risk of infant botulism, avoid giving honey — even a tiny taste — to children under the age of 1 year.

Iatrogenic botulism

To prevent iatrogenic botulism, be sure to go to a licensed health care provider for any cosmetic or medical procedures using various forms of botulinum toxin. They include onabotulinumtoxinA (Botox), abobotulinumtoxinA (Dysport) and others.

Prevention of outbreaks.

Prevention

Prevention of foodborne botulism is based on good practice in food preparation particularly during heating/sterilization and hygiene. Foodborne botulism may be prevented by the inactivation of the bacterium and its spores in heat-sterilized (for example, retorted) or canned products or by inhibiting bacterial growth and toxin production in other products. The vegetative forms of bacteria can be destroyed by boiling but the spores can remain viable after boiling even for several hours. However, the spores can be killed by very high temperature treatments such as commercial canning.

Commercial heat pasteurization (including vacuum packed pasteurized products and hot smoked products) may not be sufficient to kill all spores and therefore the safety of these products must be based on preventing bacterial growth and toxin production. Refrigeration temperatures combined with salt content and/or acidic conditions will prevent the growth of the bacteria and formation of toxin.

The WHO Five Keys to Safer Food serve as the basis for educational programmes to train food handlers and educate the consumers. They are especially important in preventing food poisoning.

The Five Keys are:

- keep clean
- separate raw and cooked
- cook thoroughly
- keep food at safe temperatures
- use safe water and raw materials.

Salmonella are a group of bacteria that can cause gastrointestinal illness and fever called salmonellosis. Salmonella can be spread by food handlers who do not wash their hands and/ or the surfaces and tools they use between food preparation steps, and when people eat raw or undercooked foods. Salmonella can also spread from animals to people. People who have direct contact with certain animals, including poultry and reptiles, can spread the bacteria from the animals to food if they do not practice proper hand washing hygiene before handling food. Pets can also spread the bacteria within the home environment if they eat food contaminated with Salmonella.

Symptoms

Most people infected with Salmonella will begin to develop symptoms 12 to 72 hours after infection. The illness, salmonellosis, usually lasts four to seven days and most people recover without treatment.

Most people with salmonellosis develop diarrhea, fever, and abdominal cramps. More severe cases of salmonellosis may include a high fever, aches, headaches, lethargy, a rash, blood in the urine or stool, and in some cases may become fatal. The U.S. Centers for Disease Control and Prevention estimated that approximately 450 persons in the United States die each year from acute salmonellosis.

Due to the range in severity of illness, people should consult their healthcare provider if they suspect that they have developed symptoms that resemble a Salmonella infection.

At-Risk Groups

Children younger than five, the elderly, and people with weakened immune systems are more likely to have severe salmonellosis infections. Learn more about People at Risk of Foodborne Illness.

Foods Linked to U.S. Outbreaks of Salmonellosis

Past U.S. outbreaks of salmonellosis have been associated with meat products, poultry products, raw or undercooked eggs and dough, dairy products, fruits, leafy greens, raw sprouts, fresh vegetables, nut butters and spreads, pet foods and treats.

Preventing Foodborne Illness at Home

Consumers should follow these steps:

- **Wash** the inside walls and shelves of the refrigerator, cutting boards and countertops, and utensils that may have contacted contaminated foods; then **sanitize** them with a solution of one tablespoon of chlorine bleach to one gallon of hot water; **dry** with a clean cloth or paper towel that has not been previously used.
- **Wash and sanitize surfaces** used to serve or store potentially contaminated products.
- **Wash hands with warm water** and soap following the cleaning and sanitation process.
- **Children, the elderly, pregnant women**, and persons with weakened immune systems should avoid eating raw sprouts of any kind.
- **People with pets** should take special care to avoid cross-contamination when preparing their pet's food. Be sure to pick up and thoroughly wash food dishes as soon as pets are done eating, and prevent children, the elderly, and any other people with weak immune systems from handling or being exposed to the food or pets that have eaten potentially contaminated food.
- Consumers can also **submit a voluntarily report**, a complaint, or adverse event (illness or serious allergic reaction) related to a food product.

Advice for Restaurants and Retailers

In the event that retailers and/or other food service operators are found to have handled recalled or other potentially contaminated food in their facilities, they should:

- **Contact their local health department** and communicate to their customers regarding possible exposure to Salmonella.
- **Wash** the inside walls and shelves of the refrigerator, cutting boards and countertops, and utensils that may have contacted contaminated foods; then **sanitize** them with a solution of one tablespoon of chlorine bleach to one gallon of hot water; **dry** with a clean cloth or paper towel that has not been previously used.
- **Wash and sanitize display cases** and surfaces used to potentially store, serve, or prepare potentially contaminated foods.
- **Wash hands with warm water and soap** following the cleaning and sanitation process.
- **Conduct regular frequent cleaning and sanitizing** of cutting boards and utensils used in processing to help minimize the likelihood of cross-contamination.

V

Food Hygiene Regulation

Food hygiene regulation: Equipment – requirement for food premises – food safety Act – Offence. Food sanitation, control & inspection: Inspection of drinking water, plant water, sewage water, equipment, cleaning, sanitizing. HACCP: Health analysis – critical control points, health of employees.

Food Safety and Hygiene Norms

It is the moral responsibility of every food business operator prevent any harm to customers. If the Food safety and hygiene norms are not followed then they may lead to foodborne disease outbreak. To prevent such incidents, World Health Organization considers Food Safety and Hygiene is Paramount. According to WHO (World Health Organization), it must include these five key Food Safety principles:

- Prevent contamination of food with pathogens
- Prevent contamination of cooked food from separate raw and cooked foods.
- Kill pathogens by cooking food for the appropriate length of time and at the appropriate temperature.

- Storage of food at proper temperatures as per the specific requirements.
- Use of potable water and safe raw materials

Every establishment dealing with the handling, processing, manufacturing, packaging, storing, and distribution of food by any food business operator should adhere to the Food Safety and Hygiene Norms. It is the responsibility of the food business operator and the persons handling food in the food establishments to ensure adherence to General hygienic and sanitary practices. This means that every food business operator shall practice steps which are critical to ensuring food safety in the activities of the food business. These procedures ensure better Food Safety and Standards Regulations.

All kinds of Food hygiene legislation in India is developed by **Food Safety and Standards Authority of India**. It is a premier organization that is administered by Ministry of Health and Family Welfare dedicated to ensuring Food Safety and Hygiene Requirements in India. Here is a list of general requirements on Hygienic and Sanitary Practices to be followed by all food business operators under the ambit of

Food Safety and Standards (**Licensing & Registration of Food Business**) Regulations, 2011:

Food Safety and Standards Regulations in India

Location and neighborhood of the food establishment: The Food and Safety Guidelines given by FSSAI suggest that it should ideally be located such that it is away from environmental pollution and industrial activities that have the potential to contaminate the food through disagreeable odor, fumes, dust, smoke, chemical emissions, pollutants. These contaminants have the potential threat of contaminating food areas prone to infestation of pests or wastes. It is also important to note that the manufacturing premises of food articles must not have any direct access to any residential area as well. Location of establishment also plays an important role in meat and meat products. In order to get a FSSAI License to any food business operator dealing in meat and meat products, one must ensure that the establishment of is linked to a meat market and is away from vegetable, fish, and other food products.

1. **Layout and design of food establishment:** General hygienic and sanitary practices include that the floors, ceilings and the walls of the food establishment must be maintained in a sound condition with no flaking and plaster. Adequate control measures must be taken to prevent insects and rodents from entering the establishment. No person shall be allowed the sale of any article within the premises of the food manufacturing unit which is not effectively separated from the place of urinal, sullage, place of storage of foul matter, or drain.

3. **Equipment and Containers:** Food hygiene guidelines suggest that all the containers used by any food establishment must be in good order and in clean hygienic conditions. These should be made of corrosion free materials. The main purpose is to protect the food from dust, dirt, flies, and insects. Appropriate cleaning and disinfecting of equipment are necessary in order to hold Food Safety and Hygiene Requirements.

4. **Facilities:** Water supply facilities must be adequate in order to ensure no risk of contamination of food articles. This means only portable water must be used as an ingredient in cooking and processing. Facilities for washing of raw materials, cleaning of utensils, drainage, and waste disposal, personal facilities and toilets, air quality and ventilation, and lighting are necessary to be developed in order to obtain a Food license for any food business operator.

5. **Food operations and controls:** Food Hygiene System must ensure that the food establishment is careful about procurement of raw materials. Expiry or use by date must be carefully checked. Temperatures for high-risk food; such as milk products,

frozen food, meat, must be maintained to ensure safe storage of raw materials and food articles.

6. **Sanitation and maintenance of establishment premises:** Proper cleaning and maintenance facilities, pest control systems must be ensured to meet **Food Safety and Standards Rules**. All food establishments must ensure a Food Hygiene System that carefully draws cleaning and sanitation programme. Specific cleaning frequencies and procedures must be set to ensure food hygiene and sanitation. Also, pest infestations shall be dealt immediately. One must be careful of not adversely affecting the food quality in the treatment of pests.

7. **Personal Hygiene:** Food Safety and Hygiene Norms must ensure personal cleanliness of the food handlers. It is the responsibility of the food business operators to provide all food handlers with Food Safety and Hygiene Requirements such as: protective clothing, head covering, face mask, gloves, and required footwear. These requirements must also be mandatory for those visiting the food establishments. Also, all food handlers must undergo regular health checkups. Any illness or disease that can be transmitted through food can be dangerous. Carriers of these diseases must not be allowed in the food establishments.

While all the Food Hygiene Guidelines have been given by Food Safety and Standards Authority of India, a food business operator must ensure that all food handlers are well aware of their roles and responsibilities in protecting food from any kind of contamination. All food handlers must be equipped with the required knowledge and skills relevant to food manufacturing, processing, packaging, storing, and serving. Food safety and quality must be ensured without any food quality deterioration.

Periodic assessments of the effectiveness of training, awareness of safety requirements, check to ensure Food Safety and Hygiene Requirements are being carried effectively are done by **Food Safety**

and Standards Authority of India.

Who must comply with this standard?

Food businesses must comply with this standard, unless they fall under the definition of 'primary food production'. FSANZ is developing primary production and processing standards separately. See the Primary Production link under "The Code" for more information on developments.

If you are a food business, whether operating from a permanent building, a vehicle or from a stall at a market, then Standard 3.2.3 Food Premises and Equipmentapplies to you. It also applies if you are selling food for a charity or for any other community fundraising project, and if you are at home and preparing food that will be sold.

However, if you are handling food in temporary premises or from home you may be able to seek an exemption from some of the requirements in this standard. For information on these exemptions you should contact your State or Territory health department or local council.

For existing premises: If you are producing food safely in your existing premises, and they met the requirements in the old food legislation or regulations for your area, it is unlikely that you will have to make any changes.

For alterations: If you are altering existing food premises any council requirements for new work will apply to your alterations and the requirements in the new standard must be taken into account.

For new premises: If you are designing and building a new food premises, you must do this in accordance with Standard Food Premises and Equipment to ensure the food business complies with the standard when it opens. If in doubt about whether your premise complies with Standard , seek advice from your local council.

What are the key provisions in this standard?

Food business premises must:

- have enough space for their equipment and the work that they do;
- be protected from pests and other contaminants such as dirt and fumes;
- be easy to clean and keep clean;
- have enough clean water available at the right temperature for the work to be done;
- have a disposal system for garbage, sewage and waste water;
- have sufficient lighting and ventilation; and
- have adequate equipment for the production of safe and suitable food.

Food business fixtures, fittings and equipment must be:

- appropriate for the work of the business;
- suitable for the jobs they are used for;
- easy to clean and, if necessary, sanitise; and
- be made of material that does not contaminate food.

Food businesses must make sure that they have:

- hand basins in work areas so staff can wash their hands in warm running water if their hands are likely to contaminate food;
- hand basins near the toilets;
- access to toilets; and
- storage areas for personal belongings and clothing, and also for the office equipment and papers and any chemicals used by the business.

Vehicles used to transport food must:

- protect the food they are carrying from contamination; and
- be designed and constructed to ensure that food contact surfaces can be cleaned and, if necessary, sanitised.

Owners must provide a food premises that:

- is easy to clean, sanitise and maintain
- is appropriate for the activities of the business
- is suitable for the jobs they are used for
- is made of material that does not contaminate food
- has sufficient space, facilities and suitable equipment to produce safe food
- provides services such as potable water, effective sewage disposal and sufficient light and ventilation for the food handling activities
- provides facilities for staff to maintain standards of personal hygiene and equipment cleanliness that will protect food from contamination
- is protected against the harbourage and entry of pests.

FSSAI Penalty and Offenses

The Food Safety and Standards Act of 2006 was established to consolidate the laws relating to food and to establish the Food Safety and Standards Authority of India (FSSAI) for laying down science-based standards for articles of food and to regulate their manufacture, storage, and distribution, sale, and import, to ensure availability of safe and wholesome food for human consumption. Therefore, to regulate the food industry, the FSSAI Act prescribes several penalties and offenses for contravening. This article will look at some of the significant FSSAI fines and violations.

Sections under which penalties are issued

The provisions relating to offenses and penalties are specified under section 48. Penalties are given from Sections 49-67 of the FSSAI Act.

Penalties for being non-compliant under the FSSAI:

Every business needs to be compliant with the laws and guidelines of the concerned authority and government. The food business needs to be compliant as it has the health of humans on its brink. The penalties under chapter 9 of the FSSAI act, there are the following sections which include the following:

Section 50: Penalty for selling food not of the nature or substance, or quality demanded

Any person who sells to the purchaser's prejudice any food which is not in compliance with the provisions of this FSSAI Act or the regulations or of the nature or substance or quality demanded by the purchaser shall be liable to a penalty not exceeding five lakh rupees.

They provided that the persons covered under sub-section (2) of section 31 shall, for such non-compliance, be liable to a penalty not exceeding twenty-five thousand rupees.

Section 51: Penalty for sub-standard food

Any person who, whether by himself or by any other person on his behalf, manufactures for sale or stores or sells or distributes or imports any sub-standard food article for human consumption shall be liable to a penalty which may extend to five lakh rupees.

Section 52: Penalty for misbranded food

Any person who, whether by himself or by any other person on his behalf, manufactures for sale or stores or sells or distributes or imports any article of food for human consumption which is misbranded shall be liable to a penalty which may extend to three lakh rupees.

The Adjudicating Officer may issue a direction to the person found guilty of an offense under this section for taking corrective action to rectify the mistake, or such article of food shall be destroyed.

Section 53: Penalty for misleading advertisement

Under chapter 9 of the Food safety and standards act, 2006, if any person publishes or is a part of a publication that advertises to falsely describes food and is possible to deceive or trick as to the nature/substance/or quality of any food or provides a dishonest guarantee, is liable to a penalty which may extend to ten lakh rupees.

Section 54: Penalty for food containing extraneous matter

Any person, whether by himself or by any other person on his behalf, manufactures for sale or stores or sells or distributes or imports any article of food for human consumption containing extraneous matter shall be liable to a penalty which may extend to one lakh rupees.

Section 55: Failure to comply with the directions of FSO

If any food business operator or importer fails to comply with the requirements under the act without any basic or reasonable ground is liable to a penalty which may extend to two lakh rupees per the directions of the Food Safety Officer.

Section 56: Penalty for unhygienic or unsanitary processing or manufacturing of food

Any person who, whether by himself or by any other person on his behalf, manufactures or processes any article of food for human consumption under unhygienic or unsanitary conditions shall be liable to a penalty that may extend to one lakh rupees.

Section 57: Possessing Adulterant

If any person themself or through any other person on his behalf, manufacture/process/imports/sells/or distributes any adulterant, is liable to the below-mentioned penalty:

- A penalty not exceeding two lakh rupees if such adulterant is not injurious to health
- A fine not exceeding ten lakh rupees if such adulterant is injurious to health

The Food Safety and Standards Authority of India (FSSAI) has recommended stringent punishment to curb food adulteration following the Supreme Court order. Those adulterating food products could face life imprisonment and a penalty of up to Rs 10 lakh as per the amendments proposed by the regulator FSSAI in its 2006 food safety and standards law.

Process for Checking Food Adulteration

The implementation and enforcement of the Food Safety and Standards Act, of 2006 rests with State Governments. Random samples of food items are drawn by the State Food Safety Officers and sent to the laboratories recognized by the FSSAI for analysis. In cases, where samples are found to contain adulterants, action is taken as per the provision of the FSSAI Act.

Powers of Food Safety Officer

A food safety officer is the authorized person to inspect the safety and security of food that is being served in restaurants or street food stalls. In case the food inspected by an officer is not fresh or had got spoilt, the FSSAI officer has all the rights to stop production of such food and issue a warning in writing to the organizer. Further, Food Safety Officer can also search or inspect any place with the help of the police force. Usually, the search is controlled or managed by a search warrant issued under the penal code.

Section 58: Contravention of FSSAI Rules

If any person who violates or opposes the rules and regulations as stated under the FSSAI act is liable to a penalty that may extend to two lakh rupees.

Section 59: Punishment for unsafe food

Any person who, whether by himself or by any other person on his behalf, manufactures for sale or stores or sells or distributes or imports any article of food for human consumption which is unsafe shall be punishable:

- Where such failure or contravention does not result in injury, with imprisonment for a term which may extend to six months and also with a fine which may extend to one lakh rupees;
- where such failure or contravention results in a non-grievous injury, with imprisonment for a term which may extend to one year and also with a fine which may extend to three lakh rupees;
- where such failure or contravention results in a grievous injury, with imprisonment for a term which may extend to six years and also with a fine which may extend to five lakh rupees;
- where such failure or contravention results in death, with imprisonment for a term which shall not be less than seven years

but may extend to imprisonment for life, and with a fine which shall not be less than ten lakh Rupees.

Section 60: Punishment for interfering with seized items

If any person illegally or without the permission of the Food Safety Officer holds/switches/transfers/or damages any such food/ vehicle/package/labeling/or advertising matter that has been confiscated, is punishable with imprisonment for a duration which may extend to six months and also with fine which may extend to two lakh rupees.

Section 61: Punishment for false information

if any person gives in false details as required under the FSSAI act is punishable with imprisonment for a duration which may extend to three months and a fine which may extend to two lakh rupees.

Section 62: Punishment for obstructing or impersonating an FSO

If any person tries to or does threaten/excuse/resist/obstruct/ intimidate/or assault the Food Safety Officer (FSO) during his checks or hours of exercising inspection is punishable with imprisonment for a term which may extend to three months and also with fine which may extend to one lakh rupees.

Section 63: Punishment for carrying out a business without an FSSAI license

If any person or food business operator (except the persons exempted from licensing under sub-section (2) of section 31 of this Act), himself or by any person on his behalf who is required to obtain a license, manufacturers, sells, stores or distributes or imports any article of food without a permit, shall be punishable with imprisonment for a term which may extend to six months and also with a fine which may extend to five lakh rupees.

Learn more about FSSAI Food Business License.

Section 64: Punishment for subsequent offenses

If any person is found guilty as per the law under the FSSAI act is again commits and is convicted of the same is liable to the following penalty-

- FSSAI license being cancelled
- An additional fine daily which may extend up to one lakh rupees, where the offense is a continuing one
- twice the punishment, which might have been imposed on a first conviction, subject to the sentence being maximum provided for the same offense

Section 65: Compensation in case injury or death of consumer

f any person themself or through any other person on his behalf, manufacture/process/imports/sell/or distributes any article of food inducing injury to the consumer or to his death, shall be lawful for the Adjudicating Officer or as the case may be, the court to direct him to pay compensation to the victim or the legal representative of the victim, a sum-

- not exceeding three lakh rupees in case of grievous injury
- not less than five lakh rupees in case of death
- not exceeding one lakh rupees in all other cases of injury

Note: The compensation is processed six months from the date of occurrence of the incident and as early as possible. If the case reaches death, an interim relief shall be paid to the next of kin within thirty days of the incident.

Section 66: Offences by Companies

The FSSAI Act prescribes the following penalties for offenses by companies –

Private Limited Companies, One Person Companies, and Limited Companies:

Suppose a company has committed an offense under the FSSAI act. In that case, every person in charge of the company when the offense was committed is held responsible and deemed guilty of the crime and shall be liable to be proceeded against and punished accordingly.

Provided that where a company has different establishments or branches or different units in any establishment or branch, the concerned Head or the person in charge of such establishment, branch, or team nominated by the company as responsible for food safety shall be liable for infringement in respect of such establishment, branch or unit:

Notwithstanding anything in sub-section (1), where a Company has committed an offense under this Act, and it is proved that the offense has been committed with the consent or connivance of or is attributable to any neglect on the part of any Director, Manager, Secretary or other Officer of the Company, such Director, Manager, Secretary or other Office shall also be deemed to be guilty of that offense and shall be liable to be proceeded against and punished accordingly.

Section 67: Imports of food in contravention of the FSSAI Act

If any person who imports any article of food which is in contravention of the provisions of this FSSAI Act, rules and regulations made there under, shall, in addition to any penalty to which he may be liable under the conditions of the Foreign Trade (Development and Regulation) Act, 1992 (22 of 1992) and the Customs Act, 1962 (52 of 1962) be also liable under the FSSSAI Act and shall be proceeded against accordingly.

Any such article of food shall be destroyed or returned to the importer if permitted by the competent authority under the Foreign Trade (Development and Regulation) Act, 1992 (22 of 1992) of the Customs Act, 1962 (52 of 1962), or any other Act, as the case may be.

Corrective actions are intended to ensure that no product injurious to health or otherwise adulterated as

a result of the deviation enters commerce. E.g., if an ingredient is involved (unsafe), it must be removed.

PRINCIPLE 6: Establish procedures for verification to confirm the effectiveness of the HACCP plan:

The HACCP system requires the preparation and maintenance of a written HACCP plan together with other documentation. This must include all records generated during monitoring of each CCP and

notations of corrective actions taken. The HACCP plan must be made on files at the food establishment

and must be made available to official inspectors upon request. the forms should provide documentation

for all ingredients, processing steps, packaging, storage and distribution.

PRINCIPLE 7: Establish documentation concerning all procedures and records appropriate to these

principles and their applications.

Validation ensures that the industry complies with the required design or plan. Industries will be

required to validate their own HACCP plans. Verification ensures the HACCP plan is adequate. It includes

reviews of CCP records, critical limits, microbial sampling and analysis.

LIMITATIONS OF HACCP:

1. HACCP requires the education of non-professional food handlers.

2. To be effective, this concept must be accepted not only by food processors but also by food

inspectors and public.

3. Experts may differ as to whether a given step is a CCP and how best to monitor such step.

WATER QUALITY MONITORING, STANDARDS AND TREATMENT

1 Water sampling

2 Testing procedures

3 Investigative analysis

4 Water treatment methods

Water sampling

1 Bore wells

2 Municipal mains

3 Water tanks and reservoirs

4 Harbour basin water

Water used for processing fish, washing fish or making ice is supposed to meet drinking water standards if it is to be considered safe. Reason: contaminated water is the main cause for pathogen-loading of fish, posing a serious health hazard to its consumer.

WHO has issued guidelines for drinking water quality, a report in three volumes. Vol. 1 deals with guideline values, Vol. 2 deals with each contaminant and Vol. 3 gives information on how to handle water supplies in small rural communities. WHO recognizes that very stringent standards cannot be used universally and so a range of guideline values for more than 60 parameters have been elaborated. Most nations have their own guidelines or standards. The control exerted by local regulatory authorities may differ from place to place depending on the local situation. So how can acceptable water quality be defined? What can the harbour-master do to ensure quality? Ensuring the quality of the harbour basin when it is contiguous with estuarine or coastal waters is perhaps beyond the scope of the harbour-master except to ensure that activities in his harbour do not add to the pollution. However, he is duty-bound to ensure that the water used for drinking, cleaning fish, ice making and fish processing meets standards of portability set in his country.

Qualitative and quantitative measurements are needed from time to time to constantly monitor the quality of water from the various sources of supply. The harbour-master should then ensure appropriate water treatment within the fishery harbour complex as well as initiate remedial measures with the suppliers when water supply from outside is polluted.

Water sampling and analysis should be done by ISO-certified laboratories. Wherever laboratories available locally are not ISO-certified, it is advisable to get their quality assessed by an ISO-certified laboratory by carrying out collaborative tests to ensure that variation in the accuracy of results is sufficiently small. Unreliable results exacerbate problems of pollution when corrective action cannot be taken in time. Sampling and monitoring tests should be carried out by qualified technicians.

Depending on the actual state of the fishing harbour infrastructure and environmental conditions in and around the harbour, monitoring should be carried out according to a specific programme for each source of water supply.

Bore wells

Contamination may arise from pollutants entering the water table some distance from the port or from sewage entering the borehole itself in the port area through cracked or corroded casings. In cases where overdrawing is evident (water is brackish), tests should be conducted at least monthly.

Municipal mains

Supply could be contaminated at source or through corroded pipelines leading to the fishery harbour. Mixing with sewage lines due to defective piping has been known to occur often. Complete tests should be carried out every half year, and the authorities should be informed when results indicate contamination.

Water tanks and reservoirs

Both types of structure are prone to bacterial growth if the residual chlorine levels in them are low or non-existent. Testing may not be necessary if periodic scrubbing is carried out. Bacteriological tests should be done at least half-yearly.

Harbour basin water

Typically, harbour basins are tested yearly. However, in areas where monsoons are very active, it may be advisable to test at the peak of the dry season when effluent point discharges tend to remain concentrated in the water body and again during the wet season when agriculture run-off may be considerable. Another critical period for harbours is the peak of the fishing season when the harbour is at its busiest and vessel-generated pollution is likely to be at its peak.

Testing procedures

1. Physical tests
2. Chemical tests

3. Bacteriological tests

While the details of sampling, testing and analysis are beyond the scope of this handbook, what follows is a general description of the significance of water quality tests usually made.

Testing procedures and parameters may be grouped into physical, chemical, bacteriological and microscopic categories.

· Physical tests indicate properties detectable by the senses.

· Chemical tests determine the amounts of mineral and organic substances that affect water quality.

· Bacteriological tests show the presence of bacteria, characteristic of faecal pollution.

Physical tests

Colour, turbidity, total solids, dissolved solids, suspended solids, odour and taste are recorded.

Colour in water may be caused by the presence of minerals such as iron and manganese or by substances of vegetable origin such as algae and weeds. Colour tests indicate the efficacy of the water treatment system.

Turbidity in water is because of suspended solids and colloidal matter. It may be due to eroded soil caused by dredging or due to the growth of micro-organisms. High turbidity makes filtration expensive. If sewage solids are present, pathogens may be encased in the particles and escape the action of chlorine during disinfection.

Odour and taste are associated with the presence of living microscopic organisms; or decaying organic matter including weeds, algae; or industrial wastes containing ammonia, phenols, halogens, hydrocarbons. This taste is imparted to fish, rendering them unpalatable. While chlorination dilutes odour and taste caused by some contaminants, it generates a foul odour itself when added to waters polluted with detergents, algae and some other wastes.

Chemical tests

pH, hardness, presence of a selected group of chemical parameters, biocides, highly toxic chemicals, and B.O.D are estimated.

pH is a measure of hydrogen ion concentration. It is an indicator of relative acidity or alkalinity of water. Values of 9.5 and above indicate high alkalinity while values of 3 and below indicate acidity. Low pH values help in effective chlorination but cause problems with corrosion. Values below 4 generally do not support living organisms in the marine environment. Drinking water should have a pH between 6.5 and 8.5. Harbour basin water can vary between 6 and 9.

B.O.D.: It denotes the amount of oxygen needed by micro-organisms for stabilization of decomposable organic matter under aerobic conditions. High B.O.D. means that there is less of oxygen to support life and indicates organic pollution.

Bacteriological tests

For technical and economic reasons, analytical procedures for the detection of harmful organisms are impractical for routine water quality surveillance. It must be appreciated that all that bacteriological analysis can prove is that, at the time of examination, contamination or bacteria indicative of faecal pollution, could or could not be demonstrated in a given sample of water using specified culture methods. In addition, the results of routine bacteriological examination must always be interpreted in the light of a thorough knowledge of the water supplies, including their source, treatment, and distribution.

Whenever changes in conditions lead to deterioration in the quality of the water supplied, or even if they should suggest an increased possibility of contamination, the frequency of bacteriological examination should be increased, so that a series of samples from well chosen locations may identify the hazard and allow remedial action to be taken. Whenever a sanitary survey, including visual inspection, indicates that a water supply is obviously subject to pollution, remedial action must be taken, irrespective of the results of bacteriological examination. For unpiped rural supplies, sanitary surveys may often be the only form of examination that can be undertaken regularly.

The recognition that microbial infections can be waterborne has led to the development of methods for routine examination to ensure that water intended for human consumption is free from excremental pollution. Although it is now possible to detect the presence of many pathogens in water, the methods of isolation and enumeration are often complex and time-consuming. It is therefore impractical to monitor drinking water for every possible microbial pathogen that might occur with contamination. A more logical approach is the detection of organisms normally present in the faeces of man and other warm-blooded animals as indicators of excremental pollution, as well as of the efficacy of water treatment and disinfection. The presence of such organisms indicates the presence of faecal material and thus of intestinal pathogens. (The intestinal tract of man contains countless rod-shaped bacteria known as coliform organisms and each person discharges from 100 to 400 billion coliform organisms per day in addition to other kinds of bacteria). Conversely, the absence of faecal commensal organisms indicates that pathogens are probably also absent. Search for such indicators of faecal pollution thus provides a means of quality control. The use of normal intestinal organisms as indicators of faecal pollution rather than the pathogens themselves is a universally accepted principle for monitoring and assessing the microbial safety of water supplies. Ideally, the finding of such indicator bacteria should denote the possible presence of all relevant pathogens.

Indicator organisms should be abundant in excrement but absent, or present only in small numbers, in other sources; they should be easily isolated, identified and enumerated and should be unable to grow in water. They should also survive longer than pathogens in water and be more resistant to disinfectants, such as chlorine. In practice, these criteria cannot all be met by any one organism, although many of them are fulfilled by coliform organisms, especially Escherichia coli as the essential indicator of pollution by faecal material of human or animal origin

.Investigative analysis

1. Test case

A harbour master's knowledge of the state of the environment in and around the fishing harbour goes a long way toward preventing outbreaks of contamination or disease with subsequent loss of resources and income. This is particularly so for the many small-to-medium fishing ports scattered around coastlines in developing countries, where, more often than not, environmental help and support from central bodies is meagre and very time-consuming.

The following is a true-life example of an investigative analysis carried out in an ASEAN country in a harbour that was experiencing problems with hygiene (coliform contaminated fish).

Test case

The port in question is situated in the mouth of an estuary. The town's water supply cannot provide the port with potable water and the port draws groundwater from a series of boreholes in and around the port area. The port's storage infrastructure consists of only one elevated concrete tank which cannot be taken out of service for cleaning. Ice is supplied by outside contractors.

Current laboratory test results were examined and found to be too consistent to reflect natural changes in the environment, pointing a finger of suspicion at the laboratory's Quality Assurance. **A new laboratory with I.S.O. certification was selected to carry out the new tests.**

Water samples were taken by external technicians from the port's borehole, the auction hall's water taps, each and every one of the external ice suppliers and the harbour basin.

A sample report from the laboratory is shown.

In this table, the first column indicates the test parameter and the last column indicates the method used to determine the test result (sometimes, more than one method may be used to determine residuals).

The second column indicates how the parameters are measured, the third column gives the actual test result which may then be compared to the values in the fourth column. The values in the fourth column are national standards or limits set by Governments and may differ from country to country. The values in the third column should not exceed those in the fourth column.

Standard Methods

A. Examination of the port's deep borehole test report revealed that whereas the iron and manganese levels were over the limit, indicating vegetable matter in the acquifer, the sodium and chloride levels were low, indicating that the pump was not overdrawing. Both the nitrate and nitrite levels were low indicating that sewage intrusion into the borehole casing was not a problem. The total bacterial count, however, was very high, indicating that the water has to be chlorinated to lower the count.

B. Examination of the auction hall's tap water test report (comparing them to the borehole water) indicates that the bacterial count is slightly lower but not enough to be considered sanitary and fit for drinking. The turbidity also dropped dramatically between borehole and tap, indicating deposition of solids inside the port's only storage tank. The nitrate level also drops as the nitrates are further converted to nitrites indicating bacteriological activity inside the overhead tank as well. As it turned out, chlorinating equipment was not installed.

C. Examination of the ice test reports reveals that both sodium and chlorides are over the limit indicating either leaking cans at the ice plants (dirty brine water enters the ice water during the chilling operation) or overdrawing at the plant's borehole. Closer examination also revealed that the nitrite levels are very high (indicating decomposed sewage) and that coliforms were present in the ice. This pointed a finger at the borehole of one particular plant, which in fact was found to be overdrawing water to meet an increase in demand. The presence of the coliforms also indicated that the ice plant's own chlorinating equipment was not functioning properly.

D. A close look at the river basin water indicated heavy contamination by sewage of the water course.

The conclusions to be drawn from the above exercise are that:

a) The most likely source of contamination was the ice supplied to the fishermen, which in turn contaminated the fish in the holds;

b) The port's own water supply and storage system was in need of an overhaul;

c) The port's river water was not to be used in any of the fish handling processes.

Gives the EU recommendations for harbour waters in general.

Harbour water is never suitable for use in fish handling processes destined for human consumption.

W.H.O. DRINKING WATER STANDARDS

PARAMETER

UNIT

LIMIT

Aluminium

mg Al/l

0.2

Arsenic

mg As/l

0.05

Barium

mg Ba/l

0.05

Berylium

ug Be/l

0.2

Cadmium

ug Cd/l

5.0

Calcium

mg Ca/l

200.0

Chromium

mg Cr/l
0.05
Copper
mg Cu/l
1.0
Iron Total
mg Fe/l
0.3
Lead
mg Pb/l
0.01
Magnesium
mg Mg/l
150.0
Manganese
mg Mn/l
0.1
Mercury
ug Hg/l
1.0
Selenium
mg Se/l
0.01
Sodium
mg Na/l
200.0
Zinc
mg Zn/l
5.0
Chlorides
mg Cl/l
250.0
Cyanide
mg Cn/l
0.1

Fluorides

mg F/l

1.5

Nitrates

mg NO_3/l

10.0

Nitrites

mg NO_2/l

-

Sulphates

mg SO_4/l

400.0

Suphides

mg H_2S/l

0

TOTAL "drins"

ug/l

0.03

TOTAL "ddt"

ug/l

1.0

Hydrocarbons

mg/l

0.1

Anionic Detergents

mg/l

0

pH

9.2

Total dissolved solids

mg/l

1500

Total hardness

mg/l

500

Alkalinity
mg/l
500
MICROBIOLOGICAL PARAMETERS
Total Bacteria
Count/ml
100
Coliform
Count/100ml
0
E. Coli
Count/100ml
0
Salmonella
Count/100ml
0
ug = microgram or ppb
mg = milligram or ppm

EU ESTUARY AND HARBOUR BASIN WATER STANDARDS

PARAMETER
UNIT
LIMIT
Mercury
ug Hg/l
0.50 (D)
Cadmium
ug Cd/l
5.00 (D)
Arsenic
mg As/l
0.50 (G)
Chromium
mg Cr/l
0.50 (G)
Copper

mg Cu/l

0.50 (G)

Iron

mg Fe/l

3.00 (G)

Lead

mg Pb/l

0.50 (G)

Nickel

mg Ni/l

0.50 (G)

Zinc

mg Zn/l

50.00 (G)

Tributyltin

ug/l

0.002

Triphenyltin

ug/l

0.008

Aldrin

ug/l

0.01

Dieldrin

ug/l

0.01

Endrin

ug/l

0.005

Isodrin

ug/l

0.005

TOTAL "drins"

ug/l

0.03

TOTAL "ddt" all 4 isomers
ug/l
0.025
para-ddt
ug/l
0.01
Hexachloro-cyclohexane
ug/l
0.02
Carbon tetrachloride
ug/l
12.0
Pentachlorophenol
ug/l
2.0
Hexachlorobenzene
ug/l
0.03
Hexachlorobutadiene
ug/l
0.10
Chloroform
ug/l
12.0
Ethylene Dichloride
ug/l
10.0
Perchloroethylene
ug/l
10.0
Trichlorobenzene
ug/l
0.40
Trichloroethylene
ug/l

10.0
Hydrocarbons
ug/l
300.0 (G)
Phenols
ug/l
50.0
Surfactants
ug/l
300.0 (G)
Dissolved Oxygen
% Saturation
80-120 (G)
pH
6-9
Sulphide
mg/l
0.04 (S)
MICROBIOLOGICAL PARAMETERS
Faecal conforms
per 100ml
2000
Total coliforms
per 100ml
10000
Salmonella
0
Entero viruses
0
ug = microgram
G = Guideline
mg = milligram
S = Suggested
D = Dissolved

2.4 Water treatment methods

- Primary treatment
- Secondary treatment
- Complete treatment

•

Treatment of raw water to produce water of potable quality can be expensive. It is advisable to determine the quantity of water needing treatment, as **not all water used in a fishery harbour or processing plant needs to be of potable quality**. Sizing of the equipment is crucial to produce acceptable water at reasonable cost. The main point to remember is that separate systems and pipelines are required for potable and non-potable water to avoid cross contamination. Each system must be clearly identified by contrasting coloured pipelines.

Water used for drinking, cleaning fish and ice-making must be free from pathogenic bacteria and may require secondary treatment or even complete treatment depending on chemical elements that need to be removed. Water for other needs like general cleaning may perhaps need only primary treatment.

Primary treatment

There are four methods of primary treatment: chlorination; ozone treatment; ultraviolet treatment; and membrane filtration.

Chlorination: Fresh or sea water can be chlorinated using either chlorine gas or hypochlorites. Chlorinated water minimizes slime development on working surfaces and helps control odour.

CHLORINATION TREATMENT

The main advantages of using chlorine gas are:

· It is the most efficient method of making free chlorine available to raw water.

· It lowers the pH of the water slightly.

· Control is simple; testing simple; and it is not an expensive method.

he main disadvantages are:

· Chlorine gas is toxic and can combine with other chemicals to form combustible and explosive materials.

· Automatic control systems are expensive.

· Chlorine cylinders may not be readily available at small centres.

· Chlorine expands rapidly on heating and hence the cylinders must have fusible plugs set at 70°C. It also reacts with water, releasing heat. Water should not therefore be sprayed on a leaking cylinder.

PERCENTAGE OF AVAILABLE CHLORINE BY WEIGHT

COMPOUND

CHEMICAL COMPOSITION

% CHLORINE BY WEIGHT

Chlorine gas

Cl_2

100.0

Monochloramine

NH_2Cl

138.0

Diochloramine

NH_4Cl_2

165.0

Hypochlorous Acid

HOCl

135.4

Calcium hypochlorite

$Ca(OCl_2)$

99.2

Hypochlorites are generally available in two forms - sodium hypochlorite solution normally available at 10% concentration and calcium hypochlorite available as a powder.

The main disadvantages of using hypochlorites are:

· Calcium hypochlorite is not stable and must be stored in air-tight drums.

· Sodium hypochlorite is quite corrosive and cannot be stored in metal containers

· Sodium hypochlorite must be stored in light proof containers.

· It is difficult to control the rate of addition of hypochlorites in proportion to water flow.

· Hypochlorites raise the pH in water.

· They are more expensive than chlorine gas.

It is important to understand the manner in which chlorine or chlorine-releasing substances behave when added to water, depending on other substances present.

· When water contains reducing substances like ferrous salts or hydrogen sulphide, these will reduce part of the added chlorine to chloride ions.

· When water contains ammonia, organic matter, bacteria and other substances capable of reacting with chlorine, the level of free chlorine will be reduced.

· If the quantity of chlorine added is sufficiently large to ensure that it is not all reduced or combined, a portion of it will remain free in the water. This is termed as residual free chlorine or free chlorine.

When chlorine reacts chemically as in the first two cases, it loses its oxidising power and consequently its disinfecting properties. Some ammoniacal chlorides however still retain some disinfecting properties. Chlorine present in this form is termed residual combined chlorine or combined chlorine.

From the standpoint of disinfection, the most important form is free chlorine. Routine analysis always aims at determining at least the free chlorine level.

Ozone treatment: Though the principle is relatively simple, this method needs special equipment, supply of pure oxygen and trained operators. Ozone is generated by passing pure oxygen through an ozone generator. It is then bubbled through a gas diffuser at the bottom of an absorption column, in a direction opposite to the flow of raw water. Retention or contact time is critical and the size of the absorption column depends on the water flow.

OZONE TREATMENT

The main advantages of ozone treatment are:

· Ozone is a much more powerful germicide than chlorine especially for faecal bacteria.

· It reduces turbidity of water by breaking down organic constituents.

· The process is easily controlled.

The disadvantages are:

· Pure oxygen may not be readily available locally.

· Ozonized water is corrosive to metal piping.

· Ozone decomposes rapidly into oxygen.

· Water has to be aerated prior to use to remove the ozone.

Ultraviolet irradiation treatment: This method is often used to treat drinking water. Successful commercial installations have been made to purify sea water in large fish processing plants.

ULTRAVIOLET IRRADIATION TREATMENT The main advantages of U-V treatment are:

· U-V rays in the range of 2500-2600 Angstrom units are lethal to all types of bacteria.

· There is no organoleptic, chemical or physical change to the water quality.

· Overexposure does not have any ill effects.

The main disadvantages are:

· Electricity supply should be reliable.

· Turbidity reduces efficiency.

· Water may require prior treatment like filtration.

· The unit requires regular inspection and maintenance.

· Thickness of the water film should not exceed 7.5 cm.

Membrane filtration: Osmotic membrane treatment methods are generally expensive for commercial scale installations. Combinations of membrane treatment with U-V treatment units are available for domestic use.

Secondary treatment

Secondary treatment of water consists of sedimentation and filtration followed by chlorination. Sedimentation can be carried out by holding the raw water in ponds or tanks. The four basic types of filtration are cartridge filtration, rapid sand filtration, multimedia sand filtration, and up-flow filtration.

Cartridge filtration: This system is designed to handle waters of low turbidity and will remove solids in the 5 to 100 micron range.

The main advantages are:

· Low cost and 'in-line' installation.

· Change of cartridge is simple.

· Operation is fool-proof. Once the cartridge is clogged, flow simply stops.

The main disadvantages are:

· Sudden increase in turbidity overloads the system.

· Cartridges may not be readily available and large stocks may be required.

Rapid sand filtration: This system consists of a layer of gravel with layers of sand of decreasing coarseness above the gravel. As solids build up on top, flow decreases until it stops. This is corrected by back-flushing the system to remove the solid build up on top

The main advantages are:

· Cost of filtration media is negligible.

· Operation is simple.

The main disadvantages are:

· A holding tank for filtered water is required to provide clear water back flushing.

· Pumping loads increase as sediments build up.

Up-flow filtration: Filtration can be at atmospheric pressure or by using a pressurised system, Figures 15a and 15b.

The main advantages are:

· High flow rates are easily attained.

· Water with turbidity up to 1500 ppm can be handled.

· Degree of filtration can be easily adjusted.

· The filter bed can be easily cleaned using the filtered water.

The main disadvantage is:

· Close supervision is necessary to ensure that the filter bed does not rupture.

Complete treatment

Complete treatment consists of flocculation, coagulation, sedimentation and filtration followed by disinfection. Flocculation and coagulation will assist in removing contaminants in the water, causing turbidity, colour odour and taste which cannot be removed by sedimentation alone. This can be achieved by the addition of lime to make the water slightly alkaline, followed by the addition of coagulants like Alum (aluminium sulphate), ferric sulphate or ferric chloride. The resultant precipitate can be removed by sedimentation and filtration.

Chemical treatment may be required to reduce excessive levels of iron, manganese, chalk, and organic matter. Such treatment is usually followed by clarification. Iron may be removed by aeration or chlorination to produce a flocculant which can be removed by filtration. Manganese may be removed by aeration followed by adjustment of pH and up-flow filtration. Most colours can be removed by treatment with ferric sulphate to precipitate the colours.

HAZARD ANALYSIS AND CRITICAL CONTROL POINT (HACCP) SYSTEM AND GUIDELINES FOR ITS APPLICATION

PREAMBLE

The first section of this document sets out the principles of the Hazard Analysis and Critical Control Point (HACCP) system adopted by the Codex Alimentarius Commission. The second section provides general guidance for the application of the system while recognizing that the details of application may vary depending on the circumstances of the food operation[1].

The HACCP system, which is science based and systematic, identifies specific hazards and measures for their control to ensure the safety of food. HACCP is a tool to assess hazards and establish control systems that focus on prevention rather than relying mainly on end-product testing. Any HACCP system is capable of accommodating change, such as advances in equipment design, processing procedures or technological developments.

HACCP can be applied throughout the food chain from primary production to final consumption and its implementation should be guided by scientific evidence of risks to human health. As well as enhancing food safety, implementation of HACCP can provide other significant benefits. In addition, the application of HACCP systems can aid inspection by regulatory authorities and promote international trade by increasing confidence in food safety.

The successful application of HACCP requires the full commitment and involvement of management and the work force. It also requires a multidisciplinary approach; this multidisciplinary approach should include, when appropriate, expertise in agronomy, veterinary health, production, microbiology, medicine, public health, food technology, environmental health, chemistry and engineering, according to the particular study. The application of HACCP is compatible with the implementation of quality management systems, such as the ISO 9000 series, and is the system of choice in the management of food safety within such systems.

While the application of HACCP to food safety was considered here, the concept can be applied to other aspects of food quality.

DEFINITIONS

Control (verb): To take all necessary actions to ensure and maintain compliance with criteria established in the HACCP plan.

Control (noun): The state wherein correct procedures are being followed and criteria are being met.

Control measure: Any action and activity that can be used to prevent or eliminate a food safety hazard or reduce it to an acceptable level.

Corrective action: Any action to be taken when the results of monitoring at the CCP indicate a loss of control.

Critical Control Point (CCP): A step at which control can be applied and is essential to prevent or eliminate a food safety hazard or reduce it to an acceptable level.

Critical limit: A criterion which separates acceptability from unacceptability.

Deviation: Failure to meet a critical limit.

Flow diagram: A systematic representation of the sequence of steps or operations used in the production or manufacture of a particular food item.

HACCP: A system which identifies, evaluates, and controls hazards which are significant for food safety.

HACCP plan: A document prepared in accordance with the principles of HACCP to ensure control of hazards which are significant for food safety in the segment of the food chain under consideration.

Hazard: A biological, chemical or physical agent in, or condition of, food with the potential to cause an adverse health effect.

Hazard analysis: The process of collecting and evaluating information on hazards and conditions leading to their presence to decide which are significant for food safety and therefore should be addressed in the HACCP plan.

Monitor: The act of conducting a planned sequence of observations or measurements of control parameters to assess whether a CCP is under control.

Step: A point, procedure, operation or stage in the food chain including raw materials, from primary production to final consumption.

Validation: Obtaining evidence that the elements of the HACCP plan are effective.

Verification: The application of methods, procedures, tests and other evaluations, in addition to monitoring to determine compliance with the HACCP plan.

PRINCIPLES OF THE HACCP SYSTEM

The HACCP system consists of the following seven principles:

PRINCIPLE 1

Conduct a hazard analysis.

PRINCIPLE 2

Determine the Critical Control Points (CCPs).

PRINCIPLE 3

Establish critical limit(s).

PRINCIPLE 4

Establish a system to monitor control of the CCP.

PRINCIPLE 5

Establish the corrective action to be taken when monitoring indicates that a particular CCP is not under control.

PRINCIPLE 6

Establish procedures for verification to confirm that the HACCP system is working effectively.

PRINCIPLE 7

Establish documentation concerning all procedures and records appropriate to these principles and their application.

GUIDELINES FOR THE APPLICATION OF THE HACCP SYSTEM

Prior to application of HACCP to any sector of the food chain, that sector should be operating according to the Codex General Principles of Food Hygiene, the appropriate Codex Codes of Practice, and appropriate food safety legislation. Management commitment is necessary for implementation of an effective HACCP system. During hazard identification, evaluation, and subsequent operations in designing and applying HACCP systems, consideration must be given to the impact of raw materials, ingredients, food manufacturing practices, role of manufacturing processes to control hazards, likely end-use of the product, categories of consumers of concern, and epidemiological evidence relative to food safety.

The intent of the HACCP system is to focus control at CCPs. Redesign of the operation should be considered if a hazard which must be controlled is identified but no CCPs are found.

HACCP should be applied to each specific operation separately. CCPs identified in any given example in any Codex Code of Hygienic Practice might not be the only ones identified for a specific application or might be of a different nature.

The HACCP application should be reviewed and necessary changes made when any modification is made in the product, process, or any step.

It is important when applying HACCP to be flexible where appropriate, given the context of the application taking into account the nature and the size of the operation.

APPLICATION

The application of HACCP principles consists of the following tasks as identified in the Logic Sequence for Application of HACCP .

1.Assemble HACCP team

The food operation should assure that the appropriate product specific knowledge and expertise is available for the development of an effective HACCP plan. Optimally, this may be accomplished by assembling a multidisciplinary team. Where such expertise is not available on site, expert advice should be obtained from other sources. The scope of the HACCP plan should be identified. The scope should describe which segment of the food chain is involved and the general classes of hazards to be addressed (e.g. does it cover all classes of hazards or only selected classes).

2. Describe product

A full description of the product should be drawn up, including relevant safety information such as: composition, physical/ chemical structure (including A_w, pH, etc.), microcidal/static treatments (heat-treatment, freezing, brining, smoking, etc.), packaging, durability and storage conditions and method of distribution.

3. Identify intended use

The intended use should be based on the expected uses of the product by the end user or consumer. In specific cases, vulnerable groups of the population, e.g. institutional feeding, may have to be considered.

4. Construct flow diagram

The flow diagram should be constructed by the HACCP team. The flow diagram should cover all steps in the operation. When applying HACCP to a given operation, consideration should be given to steps preceding and following the specified operation.

5. On-site confirmation of flow diagram

The HACCP team should confirm the processing operation against the flow diagram during all stages and hours of operation and amend the flow diagram where appropriate.

6. List all potential hazards associated with each step, conduct a hazard analysis, and consider any measures to control identified hazards

7. Determine Critical Control Points

PRINCIPLE 1

The HACCP team should list all of the hazards that may be reasonably expected to occur at each step from primary production, processing, manufacture, and distribution until the point of consumption.

The HACCP team should next conduct a hazard analysis to identify for the HACCP plan which hazards are of such a nature that their elimination or reduction to acceptable levels is essential to the production of a safe food.

In conducting the hazard analysis, wherever possible the following should be included:

- the likely occurrence of hazards and severity of their adverse health effects;
- the qualitative and/or quantitative evaluation of the presence of hazards;
- survival or multiplication of microorganisms of concern;
- production or persistence in foods of toxins, chemicals or physical agents; and,
- conditions leading to the above.

The HACCP team must then consider what control measures, if any, exist which can be applied for each hazard.

More than one control measure may be required to control a specific hazard(s) and more than one hazard may be controlled by a specified control measure.

PRINCIPLE 2

There may be more than one CCP at which control is applied to address the same hazard. The determination of a CCP in the HACCP system can be facilitated by the application of a decision which indicates a logic reasoning approach. Application of a decision tree should be flexible, given whether the operation is for production, slaughter, processing, storage, distribution or other. It should be used for guidance when determining CCPs. This example of a decision tree may not be applicable to all situations. Other approaches may be used. Training in the application of the decision tree is recommended.

If a hazard has been identified at a step where control is necessary for safety, and no control measure exists at that step, or any other, then the product or process should be modified at that step, or at any earlier or later stage, to include a control measure.

8. Establish critical limits for each CCP

PRINCIPLE 3

Critical limits must be specified and validated if possible for each Critical Control Point. In some cases more than one critical limit will be elaborated at a particular step. Criteria often used include measurements of temperature, time, moisture level, pH, A_w, available chlorine, and sensory parameters such as visual appearance and texture.

9. Establish a monitoring system for each CCP

SEE PRINCIPLE 4

Monitoring is the scheduled measurement or observation of a CCP relative to its critical limits. The monitoring procedures must be able to detect loss of control at the CCP. Further, monitoring should ideally provide this information in time to make adjustments to ensure control of the process to prevent violating the critical limits. Where possible, process adjustments should be made when monitoring results indicate a trend towards loss of control at a CCP. The adjustments should be taken before a deviation occurs. Data derived from monitoring must be evaluated by a designated person with knowledge and authority to carry out corrective actions when indicated. If monitoring is not continuous, then the amount or frequency of monitoring must be sufficient to guarantee the CCP is in control. Most monitoring procedures for CCPs will need to be done rapidly because they relate to on-line processes and there will not be time for lengthy analytical testing. Physical and chemical measurements are often preferred to microbiological testing because they may be done rapidly and can often indicate the microbiological control of the product. All records and documents associated with monitoring CCPs must be signed by the person(s) doing the monitoring and by a responsible reviewing official(s) of the company.

10. Establish corrective actions

PRINCIPLE 5

Specific corrective actions must be developed for each CCP in the HACCP system in order to deal with deviations when they occur.

The actions must ensure that the CCP has been brought under control. Actions taken must also include proper disposition of the affected product. Deviation and product disposition procedures must be documented in the HACCP record keeping.

11. Establish verification procedures

PRINCIPLE 6

Establish procedures for verification. Verification and auditing methods, procedures and tests, including random sampling and analysis, can be used to determine if the HACCP system is working correctly. The frequency of verification should be sufficient to confirm that the HACCP system is working effectively. Examples of verification activities include:

- Review of the HACCP system and its records;
- Review of deviations and product dispositions;
- Confirmation that CCPs are kept under control.

Where possible, validation activities should include actions to confirm the efficacy of all elements of the HACCP plan.

12. Establish Documentation and Record Keeping

PRINCIPLE 7

Efficient and accurate record keeping is essential to the application of a HACCP system. HACCP procedures should be documented. Documentation and record keeping should be appropriate to the nature and size of the operation.

Documentation examples are:

- Hazard analysis;
- CCP determination;
- Critical limit determination.

Record examples are:

- CCP monitoring activities;
- Deviations and associated corrective actions;
- Modifications to the HACCP system.

An example of a HACCP worksheet is attached as Diagram 3.

TRAINING

Training of personnel in industry, government and academia in HACCP principles and applications, and increasing awareness of consumers are essential elements for the effective implementation of HACCP. As an aid in developing specific training to support a HACCP plan, working instructions and procedures should be developed which define the tasks of the operating personnel to be stationed at each Critical Control Point.

Cooperation between primary producer, industry, trade groups, consumer organizations, and responsible authorities is of vital importance. Opportunities should be provided for the joint training of industry and control authorities to encourage and maintain a continuous dialogue and create a climate of understanding in the practical application of HACCP.

LOGIC SEQUENCE FOR THE APPLICATION OF HACCP

EXAMPLE OF A HACCP WORKSHEET

The Principles of the HACCP System set the basis for the requirements for the application of HACCP, while the Guidelines for the Application provide general guidance for practical application.

Since the publication of the decision tree by Codex, its use has been implemented many times for training purposes. In many instances, while this tree has been useful to explain the logic and depth of understanding needed to determine CCPs, it is not specific to all food operations, e.g. slaughter, and therefore it should be used in conjunction with professional judgement, and modified in some cases.

Why implement HACCP? It is a preventive approach to ensure food safety. End product inspection and testing, although important, is time consuming, expensive and detects the problems only after they occur. In contrast, HACCP enables us to detect hazards at any stage of processing or manufacture in order to ensure a good quality end product, by taking appropriate action at the stage where the problem occurs. It enables producers, processors, distributors and exporters to utilise resources efficiently and in a cost effective manner for assuring food safety. FSSA, 2006 places primary responsibility for safe food with producers and suppliers through HACCP, GMP, GHP. This is important for consumer protection and international food trade. It assures consistently good quality products. Scope India is experiencing growth in the area of food processing. The food industry in India accounts for about 26 per cent of the gross domestic product (GDP) and will be one of the major growth areas in the years ahead. This has given impetus to international trade but has also increased the responsibility to achieve appropriate level of safety in terms of sanitary and phyto-sanitary protection. Further, the Indian Food Safety and Standards Act of 2006, reflects a major shift in food laws and seeks to provide greater consumer protection by ensuring safety and wholesomeness of food at all stages of the food chain. This changing scenario has widened the scope and increased career options/opportunities in this area. Professionals who take up careers in this area need to have adequate knowledge and expertise in Food Chemistry, Food Processing and Preservation, Food Analysis and Quality Control. It is also desirable to be well versed in Food Microbiology, Food Laws and Sensory Evaluation. Professionals may be employed with regulatory and public health agencies as food legislators, food safety officers (inspectors), food analysts/ public analysts. Professionals can also work in voluntary agencies such as Agmark, BIS, as well as in the Quality Control Laboratories. One can work as food auditor after undergoing required training. Further, large food industries, flight kitchens, etc. have in-house quality control units which require trained professionals. In a Food Industry, numerous opportunities are available as One can initiate entrepreneurship activities through analytical food laboratory, food safety consultancy and Food Safety and Sanitation Education. Placement options are emerging at different levels in both regulatory and health agencies. Integrated approaches in Home Science curriculum, especially in the discipline of Food Science and Nutrition, impart the knowledge to improve safety and quality. The courses enable to develop skills necessary to understand and manage food safety hazards.

Food Standards Effective food standards and control systems are required to integrate quality into every aspect of food production and service, to ensure the supply of hygienic, wholesome food as well as to facilitate trade within and between nations. There are four levels of standards which are well coordinated. a. Company Standards: These are prepared by a Company for its own use. Normally, they are copies of National Standards. b. National Standards: These are issued by the national standards body, Food Safety and Standards Authority of India (FSSAI). 2022-23 . Regional Standards: Regional groups with similar geographical, climate, etc. have legislation standardisation bodies. d. International Standards: The International Organisation for Standardisation (ISO) and Codex Alimentarius Commission (CAC) publish international standards. Food Standards and Regulations in India Voluntary product certification: There are voluntary grading and marking schemes such as ISI mark of BIS and Agmark. The Bureau of Indian Standards (BIS) deals with standardisation of various consumer goods including food products and runs a voluntary certification scheme known as 'ISI' mark for processed foods. Agmark is a voluntary scheme of certification of agricultural products (raw and processed) for safeguarding the health of consumers. Since the government had several regulations and laws, food industry found it cumbersome to adhere to. A need was therefore felt to integrate all such laws for regulating the quality of food. With this in view, Indian Government has passed Food Safety and Standards Act (FSSA), 2006, to bring the different pieces of legislation pertaining to food safety under one umbrella. Food Safety and Standards Act, 2006: The objects of the Act are to consolidate the laws relating to food. The Food Safety and Standards Authority of India (FSSAI) has been established under Food Safety and Standards, 2006, which consolidates various acts and orders that have hitherto handled food related issues in various Ministries and Departments. The Food Safety and Standards Authority of India was established for laying down science-based standards for food and to regulate their manufacture, storage, distribution, sale and import, to ensure availability of safe and wholesome food for human consumption. The Act has provisions for maintenance of hygienic conditions in and around manufacturing premises, assessment and management of risk factors to human health in a scientific manner, which were not specified in the PFA. The FSSA reflects the international shift in food laws, from compositional standards or vertical standards to safety or horizontal standards. Food Safety and Standards Authority of India (FSSAI) has been mandated by the Food Safety Standards Act, 2006 for performing the following functions: • Framing of regulations to lay down the standards and guidelines for articles of food and system of enforcing various standards.International Organisations and Agreements in the Area of Food Standards, Quality, Research and Trade Since ancient times, governing authorities the world over, have made attempts to develop and implement food standards in order to protect health of consumers and prevent dishonest practices in sale of food. There have been several international organisations and agreements which have played a role in enhancing food safety, quality and security, facilitating research and trade. The major organisations which are playing a key role are:

1. Codex Alimentarius Commission (CAC)
2. International Organisation for Standardisation

3. World Trade Organisation

1. Codex Alimentarius Commission CAC is an intergovernmental body formed with the objective of establishing international standards to protect the health of the consumers and facilitate · Laying down mechanisms and guidelines for accreditation of certification bodies for certification of food safety management system for food businesses and accreditation of laboratories and notification of the accredited laboratories. · To provide scientific advice and technical support to Central Government and State Governments for framing the policy and rules related to food safety and nutrition. · Collect and collate data regarding food consumption, incidence and prevalence of biological risk, contaminants in food, residues of various contaminants in food products, identification of emerging risks and introduction of rapid alert system. · Creating an information network across the country so that the public, consumers, Panchayats, etc., receive rapid, reliable and objective information about food safety and issues of concern. · Provide training programmes for persons who are involved or intend to get involved in food businesses. · Contribute to the development of international technical standards for food, sanitary and phyto-sanitary standards. · Promote general awareness about food safety and food standards food and agricultural trade. In 2017, the membership of Codex was 187 member countries and one Member Organisation (European Community) respectively. India is a member through the Ministry of Health and Family Welfare. CAC has become the single most important international reference point for developments associated with food standards. The document published by the CAC is Codex Alimentarius which means 'Food Code' and is a collection of internationally adopted Food Standards. The document includes Standards, Codes of Practice, Guidelines and other recommendations in order to protect consumers and ensure fair practices in food trade. Different countries use Codex Standards to develop national standards. The Prevention of Food Adulteration Act 1954 (PFA, 1954) was enacted by the Government of India to

prevent adulteration of food. The Act has been amended over 200 times as per need. In addition to PFA, there are other Orders or Acts that help to ensure the quality of specific foods such as: • Fruit and Vegetable Product Order: Specifications for fruit and vegetable products are laid down. • Meat Food Products Order: Processing of meat products is licensed under this order. • Vegetable Oil Products Order: Specifications for vanaspati, margarine and shortenings are laid down. All such acts have been consolidated under the Food Safety and Standards Act. All food products manufactured in India, or imported and sold in India have to meet the requirements prescribed under the Food Safety and Standards Act.

2. International Organisation for Standardisation (ISO) The International Organisation for Standardisation (ISO) is a worldwide, non-governmental federation of national standards bodies (ISO member bodies). The mission of ISO is to promote the development of standardisation and related activities in the world with a view to facilitate the international exchange of goods and services, and to develop cooperation in the spheres of intellectual, scientific, technological and economic activity. The work done by ISO results in international agreements which are published as International Standards. ISO 9000 is an international reference for quality requirements. It is concerned with "Quality Management" of an organisation. Adoption of these standards is voluntary. The difference between Codex and ISO are given in the box given Describe current standard industrial practices. For more information visit http.www.iso.org

3. World Trade Organisation (WTO) WTO was established in 1995. The main objective of WTO is to help trade flow smoothly, freely, fairly and predictably, by administering trade agreements, settling trade disputes, assisting countries in trade policy issues. The WTO Agreement covers goods, services and intellectual property. In order to enforce adoption and implementation of standards, there is a need for a strong Food Control System. An effective food control system must consist of — (i) Food Inspection and (ii) Analytical capability. Food Inspection: Conformity of products to standards

is verified through inspection. This will ensure that all foods are produced, handled, processed, stored and distributed in compliance with regulations and legislation. Government / Municipal authorities appoint food inspectors to investigate the status of quality conformity to standards in their laboratories. Analytical capability: There is need for well-equipped, state-of-the-art accredited laboratories to carry out analysis of food. Further, well-trained personnel having knowledge of principles of laboratory management and physical, chemical and microbiological analysis of food, test foods and food products are also required. A broad range of analytical capabilities is required for detecting food contaminants, environmental chemicals, biotoxins, pathogenic bacteria, food-borne viruses and parasites. Food Safety Management Systems Over the years, issues related to food safety and quality have gone beyond just the avoidance of food-borne pathogens, chemical toxicants and other hazards. A food hazard can enter/come into the food at any stage of the food chain, therefore, adequate control throughout the food chain is essential. Food safety and quality can be ensured through. It enables to minimise or eliminate contamination and false labelling, thereby protecting the consumer from being misled and helping in purchasing products that are not harmful. GMP is a good business tool that helps to refine compliance and performance by the manufacturers/ producers. Good Handling Practices indicate a comprehensive approach from the farm to the store or consumer, in order to identify potential sources of risk and indicates what steps and procedures are taken to minimise the risk of contamination. It ensures that all persons who handle food have good hygiene practices. Hazard Analysis Critical Control Point (HACCP) HACCP is a means of providing assurance about safety of food. HACCP is an approach to food manufacture and storage in which raw materials and each individual step in a specific process are considered in detail and evaluated for its potential to contribute to the development of pathogenic micro organisms or other food hazards. It involves identification of hazards, assessment of chances of occurrence of hazards during each step /stage in the food chain — raw material procurement, manufacturing, distribution, usage of food products and defining measures for hazard(s) control.

EPILOGUE

Chef Sathishkumar Somasundaram as the Culinary Director with Green apples Food and catering. He has with over 19 years of expertise in the culinary field and has worked with Hotel industry

A dynamic epicurean, Sathish is on a quest to explore quirky and unusual ingredients to offer guests an extraordinary dining experience. His forte lies in crafting innovative creations and infusing unique flavours in conventional dishes.

Chef Sathishkumar Somasundaram is from Coimbatore, however, has travelled across multiple locations across the country and aboard, as his father served the Education department of Tamil Nadu. He also enjoys participating in Cookery. Like many authors who wrote about Food Safety in Kitchen before me, I want to express my thanks and admiration to the group of visionaries who invented Food Safety in Kitchen and to those who keep extending it creatively and applying it to new domains. I am very grateful to the many readers of the preliminary forms of the manuscript who taught me a lot by their criticism and suggested ideas that are now implemented in the text. I am also obliged to my students whose blank looks alerted me to inappropriate presentation strategies and whose improvements of classroom examples served to improve the text.

www.ingramcontent.com/pod-product-compliance
Ingram Content Group UK Ltd.
Pitfield, Milton Keynes, MK11 3LW, UK
UKHW021702190726
13853UKWH00001B/397

9 798889 517504